A Virginia Village

by

Sally Fairfax (Chinn) Reisinger

Illustrated by the Author
Howard W. Reisinger, Jr., Editor

Copyright © 2019 by Howard W. Reisinger, Jr.

All rights reserved. No parts of this book may be reproduced in any form or by any means, electronic or mechanical, including photocopying or by any information storage or retrieval system, without written permission from Howard W. Reisinger, Jr.

International Standard Book Number
978-0-578-61677-3

Library of Congress Catalogue Card Number
2020903318

Front Cover Photo
"Chinn House"
by Howard W. Reisinger, Jr.
September 2019

Back Cover Photo
Sally Reisinger
from the archives of
Howard W. Reisinger, Jr.

First Printing, April 2020
Second Printing, September 2022

Published in the United States of America

by

Howard W. Reisinger, Jr,
"Little Edge Hill"
P.O. Box 655
230 Jeannette Dr.
Tappahannock, VA 22560

Printed in the United States by
Barbour Printing
206 Prince Street
Tappahannock, VA 22560

Sharing my Mother's Memories from "Back in the Day"

To my son

Howard William Reisinger, Jr.

INTRODUCTION

The Northern Neck

Between the yellow Rappahannock
    And the broad Potomac blue
There's a lovely bit of country
    Down in old Virginia true.

Just a narrow strip of land
    On the map it's scarce a speck
But it's home to everybody
    In the good old Northern Neck.

You go sixty miles from nowhere
    Down a winding country road
Past a picturesque old mill pond
    And a patriot's first abode.

Yes, it's rather isolated,
    But I know when you reflect
You will surely want to linger
    In the good old Northern Neck.

You'll find many stately mansions
    Of the true colonial style
Tucked behind old fashioned gardens
    Filled with flowers all the while.

River views, with steamboat landings,
    Everything you could expect
Of Virginia's rich tradition
    In the good old Northern Neck.

The folks have got a charming way
    Of saying, "Come right in."
There's smoke-cured ham and batter bread
    With potatoes in the bin.

> The people still believe in God,
> And home is not a wreck
> And everybody's "kith and kin"
> In the good old Northern Neck.
>
> Sure, I've heard them sing of Heaven,
> Guess 'twas never meant for me,
> But sometimes I stop and wonder
> How the next world's going to be.
>
> But St. Peter needn't worry
> When I'm cashing in my check
> For my soul will stay forever
> In the good old Northern Neck.
>
> James B. Allen
> July 20, 1925

What could be a better introduction to the Northern Neck than this simple verse written by a young minister who spent many summers in our isolated village. Fresh from the Episcopal Seminary, vibrant, young, enthusiastic, Jim fell in love with our country and its people, as did most who came to know this tranquil land. Bordered by the Potomac and Rappahannock Rivers, it's southernmost shore washed by the magnificent Chesapeake Bay, this remote peninsula is steeped in history, rich in farmlands and forests, abounding in seafood. Much has been written about the Northern Neck, the names of its illustrious sons enshrined forever in the pages of history.

This, however, is a simple journal about a simple place and its way of life.

FOREWORD

Before my mother died in 1998 at the age of 92, I made a commitment to myself to publish her stories of growing up in the small village of Warsaw, Virginia. She was first of all a devoted wife and mother. No one who really knew her could fail to love her and find her most interesting, and above all, a true Southern lady. She was an extremely modest person who would not have believed her writing worthy of commanding the attention of anyone outside of her immediate family. I beg to differ.

Beginning in middle age, she wrote these stories over many years. I can see her now with her pad of foolscap, patiently pouring out from her heart what she called her "picture memories": vivid vignettes of a simple but rich life in a very different era, the whole suffused with the deep and abiding love of family and friends. Suffering from macular degeneration in the last twenty years of her life, she wrote well beyond her ability to see what she was applying to paper, guiding her writing hand with the other in an attempt to control her increasingly illegible handwriting.

My mother was one of five children of Justice Joseph William Chinn and his wife, Sally Douglas Chinn. She relates in these chapters the places and people of her youth, what they wore, what they valued, how they expressed themselves. The story was written out of what she had gleaned from her life that was important. Her descriptions often will be unfamiliar to those of the present generation, and some parts may not be considered "politically correct" by today's standards. In my light editing to prepare these stories for publication, I have made every effort to leave her style and expression intact. For this I make no apologies, since indeed therein lies much of the beauty and attraction of what she wrote.

My mother was a true artist on many levels. Painting, poetry and music—both classic and popular—defined much of her life. Until she lost her eyesight, she was a fine portrait painter, dividing her time between her family and art. The portrait of which she was most proud was one she painted of her father that hangs in the Virginia Supreme Court Building in Richmond. A glimpse of her artistic skills appears in the simple sketches that she created to accompany this little book. She loved poetry, too, from the time she was a little girl, and committed reams of verse to memory. She could amaze family and friends by reciting lengthy poems by heart right up until the last days of her life. Not only does this little book include a few of her poems; her prose, too, frequently is touched by the poetry of her soul. My mother's love of music and singing often gives a lilting presence to her sensuous descriptions of even the most mundane of observations.

I want to thank The Northern Neck News for the important role that this newspaper played in my mother's memories and writing. While every effort was made to quote faithfully from this much loved newspaper, I beg forgiveness if there are any errors in this work. Some of the articles indeed could not be found and likely may have been completed in part from my mother's memory. My mother also sometimes struck out actual names mentioned in the articles in her desire to offend no one. I also want to thank my dear wife, Joyce (Milby) (Green) Reisinger, a family friend for many years prior to our marriage in 2014, for her indefatigable help and encouragement that were my strongest inspiration to complete this publication.

FOREWORD

In closing, I call to mind just how vast the changes have been since my mother's youth. The Chinn House in which my mother and her siblings grew up now is the heart of the Rappahannock Community College. The Chinn family is proud of the part they played in assuring that this house in its new role continues to be a welcoming presence in the community. But perhaps of even greater significance is the simple but extraordinarily rich family life that has faded from our society along with the laughter of those little children playing their simple games in this home and village of so long ago. These vignettes offer in their way a nostalgic glimpse into the life of a family and village that now live on only in the realms of memory.

Howard W. Reisinger, Jr.
July 2020

A VIRGINIA VILLAGE

CONTENTS

Chapter		Page
	INTRODUCTION	*v*
	FOREWORD	*vii*
	CONTENTS	*xi*
1	THE VILLAGE	*1*
2	LOCAL COLOR	*5*
3	CAREFREE DAYS	*9*
4	EARLY FRIENDS	*15*
5	FINE FEATHERS	*21*
6	THE ART OF LEARNING	*25*
7	PICTURE MEMORIES	*31*
8	IPECAC AND THINGS	*35*
9	BEGINNINGS	*41*
10	A BIT OF ENGLAND	*47*
11	DIFFERENT PEOPLE	*53*
12	BOUNTY	*57*
13	MAMMY	*61*
14	THE HOUSE NEXT DOOR	*67*
15	THE LAST OF PEA-TIME	*69*
16	KITH AND KIN	*77*
17	INTERIM DAYS	*83*
18	NORTHERN NECK NEWS	*89*
19	GROWING PAINS	*93*
20	STORY BOOK HOUSE	*99*
21	ORGAN MUSIC	*105*
22	MISS SALLY	*109*
23	CHRISTMAS	*113*
24	FRINGE BENEFITS	*119*
25	WASHINGTON SLEPT HERE	*123*
26	THE VILLAGE CHURCH	*125*
27	THE JUDGE	*131*
28	COURT DAYS	*135*
29	THE GIRLS	*141*
30	ENTERTAINMENT	*145*
31	THE COLONEL	*153*
	CONCLUSION	*159*

1

THE VILLAGE

It was a friendly little village with a dirt road through the center, jutting off at an angle to form its one corner. It laid claim to two general stores, the likes of which supplied many needs for those in the village and thereabout. Within these frame buildings, long wooden counters displayed an assortment of homely household commodities: china in broken lots, feather dusters, lamp chimneys, chewing tobacco, stone crocks, machine oil—countless mundane necessities to do with country living. It was here, too, one could buy yard goods from bolts of snowy muslin and gay percale, neatly stacked on open shelves alongside trimmings of Val lace, ruffles of Swiss embroidery and Irish crochet. A well-worn yardstick hung conveniently from a nearby nail, and sewing threads of many colors filled the narrow drawers of the familiar spool cabinets.

In a small showcase to the back of the room, one found frames of golden honey and prints of country butter wrapped in tissue paper or cheese cloth, and from the counter top, the redolent odor of a big cheese seeped from beneath the lid of a slatted box. Bulging glass jars contained tantalizing candy: fat red striped peppermints, licorice sticks, lemon and horehound drops, while slant topped bins offered ginger snaps and frosted cakes through their glass windows. There come to mind barrels of grist from a local mill, and a ponderous drum of black molasses, a tin can beneath its spigot to catch the sticky drip. This is the way it was, remembering those country stores with their smell of kerosene, salt herring, and oily leather harness: a potpourri of odors impregnating the tobacco filled air.

A VIRGINIA VILLAGE

The proprietor and owner of one such business was "Old Harry," as he was known affectionately, a slight man with somber black eyes and a drooping black moustache. Any description of him would be incomplete without noting the shapeless felt hat pulled down about his ears. Worn constantly both indoors and out, it was as much a part of him as his unpressed suit of nondescript brown. But, of far greater importance, "Old Harry" held a special place in the affections of all who knew him, as well as an enviable reputation for his kindness and integrity. There was always an inch or two added to the measure of yard goods, an extra ounce to the weight of sugar in the splotched metal scales, extra lumps of candy in the brown paper bag—for "good measure." As a small girl I often accompanied my friend, Lucy, to his back office, when she would beg candy from "Daddy" for the two of us. Sitting before his roll-top desk with its confusion of papers and unrelated things, he would pretend he did not see us. We waited, however, patiently . . knowingly . . for the inevitable moment when he would rise, reach for a small paper bag, and make his way to the candy barrel.

In the cool shade beneath the raised porch on the front of the building, village dogs sought refuge from summer's heat, while on the narrow bench above, the village loafers spit tobacco juice and expounded their doubtful philosophies. They moved inside with the coming of winter—moved in to the circle of heat radiating from the pot bellied stove, a brass spittoon conveniently near and horse collars hanging above.

In addition to the general store, the village proper consisted of the usual small businesses—places such as a pool parlor, an uninviting lunchroom, and a first rate bank. There was Uncle Tom's butcher shop and Mr. Garland's ice cream parlor. The latter, a tiny building by the side of the dirt sidewalk, was a popular place for young and old when it opened twice a week.

THE VILLAGE

The in between days were needed for making the large freezers of ice cream, with peaches from a local orchard, strawberries from a special patch, to say nothing of velvety banana, smooth, rich chocolate, and satisfying vanilla. There was surely no greater bliss than that first delectable lick from the top of the cone, piled high with incomparable deliciousness . . . a whole nickel's worth!

Uncle Tom's butcher shop, a small weathered building with an abundance of dusty growth about its sagging porch, was of equal importance, for Uncle Tom butchered and sold fresh meats. He also cut hair in the room behind the pool parlor. Aside from these worthy accomplishments, Uncle Tom held a place of no little importance with the village children, for it just so happened he had the steepest, most treacherous hill for coasting behind his neat, frame house. Only the most experienced and the most daring braved that snow packed terrain. Lastly, Uncle Tom, heavy of build, thick of jowl, claimed another distinction. Although his education was limited, it was generally known he could add a column of figures in his head without the use of pencil and pad. As a result, Uncle Tom vowed to leave his head to science. As a child, I carried the frightening image of a headless Uncle Tom.

Plumb center of the village was its only two story public building—an ugly square edifice known as the bank building, housing a drug store on the left, the bank on the right. The second floor consisted of offices of one kind or another; and it was up the steep, dimly lit stairs that my father once had his law office. Ambition, along with the needs of a growing family, often induced him to burn the midnight oil, not taking time to return for the evening meal. It was then that my mother would send his dinner on a big tray, covered with a large, linen napkin, carried by the faithful Walter down the dirt walk and up the steep stairs.

A VIRGINIA VILLAGE

Men in this village usually walked to and from their offices or places of business, usually encountering friends and neighbors along the way. There was always time to stop briefly, exchange news of local happenings, and speak of headlines from a city newspaper received in the morning mail. At home, there was time for wives to visit over neighboring fences, arrange perhaps a foursome of bridge for the evening, with light refreshments to enhance the simple occasion: pound cake with ambrosia, sponge cake, and lemonade on a summer's night; but come winter, plum pudding with steaming coffee, oyster stew, and country sausage.

It seemed that nothing of far reaching importance ever happened in this village, nestling between two rivers in the Virginia countryside. Not harried, free of the frenzied competition of a metropolitan center, the people lived each day for what it brought. They lived in a simple complacency and delightful inertia. To use their own expression, "beyond a shadow of a doubt," life in their village had its compensation.

2
LOCAL COLOR

The arrangement of the village, as you might guess, was in no way planned; rather, places sprang up where it seemed a likely place to be. A walk down either of the two roads, bordered in part by dirt sidewalks and shaded by overhanging trees, would take you past familiar houses and yards, with here and there open fields where horses and cattle grazed. In my mind's picture, each familiar place had some special characteristic that identified it with those who lived there. It was, as an example, a round turret on the tall frame house that I identified with the Sydnors. It was the iron fence about the Jones property, the picket fence around the Tyler house, and two ivy covered trees at each side of the gate at the Segar house. It was a high front porch on the Wellford house, the privet hedge around Cousin John's; and when one thought of Miss Annie Brown on the far side of the village, one thought of her neat white cottage behind a clapboard fence, and the mimosa tree in the kitchen yard. This is the way it was remembering the village, these and other places forming a part of the whole.

But to speak of the physical aspects of the place would be dull indeed without meeting some of the people. Within the perimeter of this small town lives touched, and they became a community family of sorts, sharing communal joys and sorrows, sharing a way of life. One might think that in such remote surroundings would be found a benighted people. Rather, theirs was a proud heritage—not a few obtaining a formal education, many excelling in their chosen fields. Geographically cut off from neighboring lands, the people of the Northern Neck relied for the most part on their own resources and their own entertainment.

A VIRGINIA VILLAGE

It was Leap Year, 1908, and the editor of our local newspaper published for his readers' enjoyment a list of the then eligible young bachelors about the village. To some this may seem bucolic, but it portrayed well thought out character sketches, freshly original and amusing. The following is that list, in part:

Eligible Young Men . . . For Matrimony

F. A. . . . , deputy clerk of Richmond County. This is a dashing and glorious chance for some lonesome maiden that needs a most pleasant companion. He owns a house and lot in the center of town with flowers in front that bow and smile to you as you pass the place. He is very attractive, handsome and deliberate in his undertakings. We can say that he is one of the best catches in our line. He is fond of hunting and all sports, and is considered good at them all.

H. G. . . . , farmer. This is a fine opportunity for a young girl that likes the outdoor life and a home that none in Virginia can surpass. He is energetic and always willing to help the women and is quite a favorite with them. He is very attractive, dances well and is fond of fox hunting. We honestly think that the lady who wins this young man's dear heart will be so fortunate, as we think him the catch of the season.

O. P. . . . , assistant cashier of the L. E. Mumford Banking Company, is a little bashful but is fond of the very young debutantes. He is very popular in general, a fine accountant, "and has got the money, too." He is willing to put the washing out. Can make fine molasses candy, a good tennis player, but does not believe in dancing. Expert at telegraphy and telephone, a fine catch for the right one.

C. M. . . ., a merchant, owns the finest driving horse in town and is a fine driver. This young man is lonesome and will be ready to kneel to the fair one who will listen to his tale of woe; he is very charming and bears a fine standing with all who know him for his congeniality.

A. N. . . . , lawyer, who can plead his cases with ease before the bar of

LOCAL COLOR

justice, but is just a little shy to argue a case pertaining to the heart. We think if the fair sex would assist him in the latter case he will surrender with all his worldly goods, etc. He is handsome, good natured and we think would make a most charming companion for life.

A. W. . . . , with the V. V. C. Company, is noted for his fine voice and piano playing; a fine dancer and thinks he can play tennis. He has been trying to get a companion for some time, but nothing doing. He is very attractive and congenial. Does not care for drink or tobacco, but is fond of the ladies. Ladies bait your hook and take him in. You will find that he will bite and real easy. He owns a fine house and lot in town on West End and all paid for.

— *Northern Neck News, 1908* (Reprinted Thurs., Feb 27, 1964, Sec 2, pg. 5)

So much for these little vignettes—some just a name, others a very real memory, a part of the past.

Just as names of people became lost over the passage of time, so also are forgotten many familiar places. Places such as Berlin's Shop, once a blacksmith's shed by the side of the road. Today, all traces of this enterprise are gone. Within the recent past, only a big oak tree marked the spot for those who remembered.

Just out from the village in yet another direction a rippling brook flowed across the road, disappearing into the woods alongside. When fording this shallow stream with horse and vehicle, it was customary to stop midway that the horse might drink the clear, cool water. Today Clark's Run is no more. It, too, is a name and place obscured by time, obliterated by nature.

It is gratifying that the lovely, picturesque Indian names, so prevalent in this area, still remain. Old houses, churches, towns, rivers, and streams—Menokin, Mattaponi, Totuskey, Yeocomico—and countless other names tied in with the early history of Tidewater Virginia. One finds, also, scattered about the countryside, many

A VIRGINIA VILLAGE

predominantly English names, brought by early ancestors from the Old World: Gloucester, Lancaster, King and Queen, Westmoreland. Nestling on the bank of the Potomac River, a small hamlet bears the Irish name, Kinsale. In recent years, the mayor of Kilmarnock, Scotland, visited our small town of that name in the Northern Neck. It is only fitting that in this historic area, where our early ancestors took root, names should bespeak an Old World origin.

But then, it piques the imagination to come upon such places as Lively, Horsehead, and Nuttsville.

3
CAREFREE DAYS

In thinking of this village, my thoughts reach back to early childhood, back to my family and home. Here I must touch briefly on those early days and growing up in the big sunny house with the sloping green yard.

One of the earliest memories centers around the nursery, a large room with big windows through which the sunlight filtered on the white spreads of double beds, and cast flickering squares of light on the woven rug. In summer, when called in from dusky twilight

and the fascinating game of catching lightening bugs, one would hear through the open windows the sounds peculiar to summer. The sounds of the distant barking of a dog, the mumble and laughter of adult voices from the porch below, and the hum of summer's insects, as well as the occasional fragrance of honeysuckle, were all brought in through the fluttering curtains. At one end of the nursery an open fire blazed merrily on a winter's evening, and a folding clothes rack stood to one side laden with fresh clothes for the morrow: long, fleecy underwear, white ribbed stockings, starched shirts, and crisp pastel dresses with matching hair ribbons.

There was a security and warmth in this room, a sense of belonging in this tranquil environment, where many hours were spent in happy, imaginative play, building fairy tale castles and stories in the glowing coals on the hearth.

We would not know about growing up in another place, only our village where everyone knew one another. Here children crossed wide yards from familiar houses set well back, for a game of "I Spy," "Devil in the Ditch," and "Fox and Geese"; the younger forming a circle for "Ring Around the Rosie," "Drop the Handkerchief," "Blind Man's Bluff," and "London Bridge." Inside the comfortable frame homes, their window shades drawn against the heavy heat of summer, parents inevitably heard the high pitched voices of children at play. Riding a stick horse was a favorite pastime when one was little and playing alone. A touch of a switch broken from the mock orange bush and one was off down imaginary roads to far away places. Rolling a hoop required less fancy and more skill—maneuvering past old ladies on sidewalks and sleeping dogs in the dusty road.

CAREFREE DAYS

There were pets of all kinds in those early days, and I remember a white bulldog with a bobbed tail, black patch over one eye and teeth protruding from a jutting jaw—but Jeff seemed docile, even affectionate. All was well until a time when housewives in the village had their poultry killed a mysterious way, and Mama, eventually, was told of like happenings in our hen lot. It was concluded to be the work of a weasel, so a trap was set at our hen house door to catch the ugly varmint. It was a dark moment, a moment of truth, to find in the morning Jeff caught in the trap.

"Wee dog" was a very special little mongrel puppy my brother found abandoned, shivering on a backcountry road. There was love at first sight, the moment he was placed, bright eyed and trusting, on the foot of my mother's bed. It was a traumatic occasion the day Wee dog disappeared, causing no few tears of distress. After many inquiries and a notice in our local paper, we learned he had been seen at a crossroad some miles away. Papa arranged his return, and it was a joyful reunion when the small sulky that carried the mail drove into our lane. At the driver's feet sat Wee dog, his small body wriggling with joy, his brown eyes shining with love at the sight of familiar faces.

"Laddie" grew from a frolicsome puppy into a lovely, white collie with silky hair, amber colored eyes, and a feathery tail. In summer, his luxurious coat was unbearably hot and he panted incessantly, drooling rivulets from the end of his pink tongue. One day my compassionate brother turned barber and Laddie was shorn of his raiment, leaving rows of scalloped white hair and pink skin. Just as Sampson when shorn of his hair lost his strength, so Laddie lost self pride, spending the rest of the summer under the hydrangea bushes. It was only when he acquired a new coat of sorts that he resumed his visits to the village drugstore to beg ice cream cones from admiring friends.

A VIRGINIA VILLAGE

There was no animal hospital in those days; there was no veterinarian. There was, however, an old man back in the countryside, known to be good with ailing farm animals. His talents, it seemed, did not include house pets. There was a real dilemma the day Laddie was struck by a car, leaving a long, open gash in his side. To me there was only one avenue of help, and I called our old family physician. "But Sal Jane," I heard him say, "I don't practice on dogs." "I know," I protested tearfully, "but it looks really bad . . . he might even die." There was a moment of silence; then, "I'll be right up, Sal Jane" was the blessed response. "Maybe a small table out back" he added, his voice trailing off. I understood. This would be a very private, a very special visit. I would not let him down.

Finally I must speak of "Punk," a big yellow cat we found in our hay barn. He, too, became an important member of our household, inspiring my first bit of doggerel at about the age of 12:

> Punk is my little cat
> > He's yellow with white paws
> If you once saw that pussycat
> > You'd wish that he was yours.
>
> He has eyes big and yellow
> > And a little pink nose
> Soft white fluffy ears
> > And cute little cushion toes
>
> He has a clean white collar
> > That he wears every day
> He stays close by me most time
> > But sometimes runs away.

CAREFREE DAYS

I like to dress my kitty
   In a baby dress and cap
And put him in the doll's bed
   When it's time to take a nap.

He looks so very funny
   With his ears all plastered down
And his long tail switching
   Below the bottom of the gown.

He feels all warm and cuddly
   And somehow I do not care
When he misbehaves and scratches
   Or hides beneath the chair.

If his eyes grow big and glisten
   While he watches for a rat
When he looks more like the jungle
   Well … I still love my yellow cat.

As we ascended the stair step ladder of childhood, we each in turn wished for a pony, which proved the one pet hard to come by. I recall a morning I was awakened by my Aunt and asked, "What do you think is in the other room?" The day before having been my birthday, it was bound to be a belated birthday present. "A pony!" I shouted. "No," she smiled, "A dear little baby sister." Who would make such a mistake as to leave a baby instead of a pony in mother's bedroom? Eventually, my little sister added "pony" to her most wanted list.

We grew up with the familiar characters in well known children's books, beginning with "Mother Goose," followed by the much loved "Peter Rabbit," "Black Beauty," "Little Lord Fauntleroy," "Uncle Remus," "Robinson Crusoe," "Hans Brinker"

... countless others: "Tom Sawyer," "Little Women," "Call of the Wild." There were, of course, all the Horatio Alger books, to say nothing of Andersen's and Grimm's fairy tales—far too many to recount.

Many parents probably form in their minds what they think their children might become when grown. So it was with ours. One of my brothers would become a lawyer, the other a doctor, carrying on the two professions predominant in our family. Both ably fulfilled these positions. My sister with the lovely voice would become an opera singer. Such a possibility was well within reason, but she turned her talents to the field of education with great success. I, who had a way with brushes and crayons, fell far short of becoming an artist, and it was generally conceded my little sister would fill an important role by just being herself.

So much for fleeting glimpses into the heart of my family, forming the warp into which the threads of my memory are woven.

4
EARLY FRIENDS

In the center of what is known as the barn lot stood our big, red barn. Here, in addition to the regular horse stalls, was a separate box stall used, I believe, for isolating a mare in foal, or a horse of fractious disposition. Conveniently near was the corncrib, and in a tack room to one side hung harness needed for riding or driving. The roomy carriage house, with its wide doorway and dirt floor, held in addition to the family carriage a sporty topless buggy called a runabout, as well as two or more of conventional design, known affectionately as "old buggy" and "new buggy." Above spread the hayloft with a ladder descending from an opening in the floor.

In the barn lot there was a silo, a shed for farm machinery and a separate shed for milking. The latter brings to mind an amusing true story once told around our village. It seems that one of our well-known citizens purchased from "down the county a way" a cow which was being brought by hoof to its new home. The kindly buyer, thinking to break the trip for man and beast, telephoned a friend who lived en route and asked if he could put up the cow and foot weary man overnight. It was agreed, and some days later the benevolent host received, in all its simple candor, the following appreciative call: "I am grateful to you, Ben, for your hospitality to my cow, and I want you to know if ever your cow wants to spend the night out, just send her right up. I'd be happy to have her."

Towering over everything in the barn lot was the tall, steel windmill. Above the water tank was the big wheel with stiffly flared blades and wind pennant to one side. Subject to the whims of nature, when dark clouds hung low on the horizon and wind swept across open fields, the windmill came alive. The big wheel would turn in rapid frenzy, causing the rod to clang in furious

A VIRGINIA VILLAGE

protest as it raced up and down, filling the water tank above. Other times it stood motionless, etched against the blue of the sky, the flanges of its blades glistening in the sunlight. There was something romantic about the tall windmill that stirred the imagination, and as a small boy my brother would climb the steep ladder to the water tank. In his mind it became a rope ladder leading to the crow's nest, and under the wind pennant sail, high in the rigging of his ship, he scanned the far horizon.

Outside the barn lot there were buildings such as a hen house, a meat house, a wood shed—the general plan of most back lots. The servants' house was yet another building, and I recall many kind persons who moved in and out of it during those early days. Perhaps it is colored Mattie I think of first—capable, raw boned Mattie—who was as adept at hitching a pair of horses to the big carriage as preparing a meal on the old cook stove in the kitchen. It was a wood range, with firebox on one side, a variety of iron plates with curved lifters on the top. Extending from the extreme top were warming ovens: shiny metal ovals bearing the name "Home Comfort." Here one might find leftovers such as a slice of pie, a roasted sweet potato, and an over sized "George biscuit." Mattie made the latter from ends of biscuit dough for George, the hired man.

EARLY FRIENDS

It was the snow covered boot of George, leaving a wet track on the kitchen floor one Christmas Eve, that caused excitement among us children as never before. Santa Claus must have been right there in our kitchen. This conclusion was made more real by Mattie's disregard for truth, in favor of stars in children's eyes. "Deed, sho nuf, he been right here," adding as an after thought, "I spec you better be special good, bein' as he close by." "What did he say?" we asked in wonderment and awe. "Seems like, he most wants to know who been good 'round here, so to know whether to plan on coming back later." In Mattie's answer to him lay all the promise for the morrow. What did she tell him? We were afraid to ask.

In those days of our early childhood, Mattie played other important roles, as in the case of the runaway buggy. Papa had engaged a carpenter from the other side of the river to do some special work about the place. With his work completed, Mr. B. was ready to be taken back to the ferry landing. Mitchell, a colored youth who did odd jobs about the barnyard, was selected to drive him. He chose "Rowdy," the high spirited, unpredictable young sorrel horse to hitch to the buggy. Unknown to anyone, my small brother had climbed into the boot of the buggy behind the seat. Soon it was discovered he was missing, and one of us children remembered seeing him leave in the back of the buggy. Without further ado, Mattie took to the road, running in an effort to catch them. Mama frantically called Eddie, who was mowing the grass with a horse drawn mower, to hook up the big bay horse, "Chester," hoping that she could catch them before they had gone too far. Very shortly, she came upon Mattie, panting on the side of the road. She raised her hand to stop Mama. "Yo needn't go no fu'ther; I'se done sont for him." Mattie had encountered a man she knew on a big black horse coming toward her. Yes, he had met the buggy with its passenger and priceless cargo. "Turn right around, go back as fast as you can, and fetch Miss Sally's child," Mattie demanded. Back home, Eddie unhooked the mare, "Annie," from the lawn mower without removing the harness. Only taking time to loop up the traces over the hames, he sat astride the harness and mare. He now joined Mama and Mattie. It was really not long before the big black horse and its rider, with a broad grin on his face, came into view. Seated close in front of him was the tiny boy, with white dress spread over the saddle.

It is not really clear how it came about, but I recall Mattie once drove us children in our big carriage to a colored baptizing. The black carriage, with isinglass windows, was not the most handsome as a carriage might be, but it was roomy and adequate for transporting the family, with its heavy velour lap robe for winter, fringed linen duster for summer. On that August day a blanket of heat enveloped the throng of spectators lining the sun drenched river shore. It reflected on the still water and glistened on the stark white sheets wrapped about the simple converts being led into the water for immersion. Here, standing waist deep, the Reverend Preacher met each glorified member of his flock with solemn admonition and prayer before dipping them in the limpid water. Rising like a great wave, the full rich voices of those along the shore rang out in emotional songs of praise and thanksgiving: old hymns, such as "Shall we gather at the River," "Safe in the Arms of Jesus," and "Rock of Ages." As I clung to Mattie's hand, my small voice was lost in the tumult.

To join the church, one need first "get religion" and surrender ones self to the Lord—a fact made more meaningful in our lives by a nurse we once had named Madgelene. Madgelene, unlike her usual self, took to spending more and more time alone in her room in the big attic above our house, appearing only when she was called. On occasions, strange sounds drifted down the narrow stairs although we knew she was alone, and there was audible conversation, accompanied by a clapping of hands and shuffling in a dance of ecstasy. We learned Madgelene was "seeking." One day all was normal again, and she had peace and was ready to "jine" the church.

I remember Hattie, who accentuated her short, plump figure by the addition of several starched petticoats beneath her stiff calico

EARLY FRIENDS

dress, covered by a white apron. And there was Ella, remembered especially for her broiled chicken, cooked in butter on top of the stove in a heavy skillet—the lid weighted down by two or more flat irons. Who could forget her strawberry shortcake, made of biscuit dough into a round hoecake, split, buttered, filled with crushed strawberries, and topped by whole berries dipped in powdered sugar? Finally, a syrup of the mashed berries was poured over the hot dessert in place of the usual whipped cream.

Then, there was old Gracie, with young ideas in spite of her toothless gums and receding hairline under the familiar white cap. Once Gracie took unto herself a young lover, one James, for whom she purchased a new pair of trousers. Things did not go well one Saturday evening when she joined the assemblage of colored folk that habitually gathered in the village. Her eye fell on James in the company of a young girl, and to add insult to injury, he had on the pants Gracie had bought him. Shaking with anger, pointing an accusing finger, she approached him shouting, "Youse, James, you take off them breaches." Heedless of snickering bystanders, she continued. "You hears me. I sez, take off them pants. Youse get outen them right now!" This story reached us by way of the grapevine, and we never learned the fateful results.

Among old colored friends was Aunt Nancy Parker, who lived with her husband by the side of the Mestermins Lane, which ran inward from the main road through the village. Her tiny, well scrubbed cabin held a constant fire on the open hearth, for Aunt Nancy cooked her meals in iron skillets over glowing coals. It so happened she owned a parrot, an aged, moth eaten bird, with a ratty tail and faded green plumage. When tired of play in our familiar surroundings, we could always go by way of the back field, behind our vegetable garden, to visit Aunt Nancy and her parrot. There, one was sure of a buttermilk biscuit, spread with molasses, while sitting atop the high bed with its freshly washed patchwork quilt, the better to watch the husky voiced old bird in its nearby cage. Once overcome with sleep,

A VIRGINIA VILLAGE

I took my afternoon nap on the high bed in the warm, safe room.

There were many other colored personages who came to us "as green as gourds" from the cornfields and back woods. Having once acquired domestic training from my mother, the lure of the big city was too strong, and they went. It is sad that such worthy friends, such respected citizens, are gone. It is sad that children today will never know an Aunt Nancy.

5
FINE FEATHERS

It is unbelievable that once Baltimore was the city most accessible to the people in the Northern Neck. Though Richmond was the nearer as the crow flies, the Rappahannock River created quite a barrier, and on the opposite side there could be difficulties, even hazards, in the unpaved road extending miles ahead to the city. From nearby landings on the river, the trip to Baltimore by steamboat was leisurely and pleasant. Yet, it was a real journey, so for the most part it was infrequent.

Some counted themselves fortunate to have relatives or friends in a city to obtain for them things not found in a country store. Clothes, if not made at home, were ordered by mail from city department stores, and a letter describing an article proved, for the most part, satisfactory. Shoes were also ordered by mail, the size determined by outlining the bare foot on a sheet of paper, sending it along with choice of style and color. . . sturdy brown oxfords, sandals, patent leather Mary Janes, etc. The spring and fall catalogs from mail order houses were eagerly thumbed through, eventually becoming the property of small girls for cutting out paper dolls.

Much of the sewing was done in the home, especially when there were children. I recall that Mrs. Settle came to our house twice a year for a stay of several weeks, completing stacks of pants and shirts for my brothers, ruffled petticoats and dresses of white muslin, trimmed with Val lace and insertions for us girls. There were pique coats with collars edged in Irish crochet, ruffled pique sunbonnets, and hats with buttoned down crowns with chinstraps. Bolts of material were gotten well in advance, and the old Singer sewing machine in the back bedroom hummed incessantly under the constant tread of the foot pedal.

We were especially fortunate to have in our village such an accomplished dressmaker as Miss Evelyn. Miss Evelyn lived in a little house near the heart of the village with Jock, her adored (if indolent) spouse. She was a real artist at sewing beautiful things. Indeed she was bound to be very special at such things, for did she not make elegant, sophisticated gowns for Cousin Claude? Cousin Claude, the wife of a prominent politician who lived in our village, kept Miss Evelyn occupied exclusively when it was about time for Congress to convene. At that time, Cousin Claude would descend on Washington for the duration and the many social affairs. It seems fantastic that the lovely clothes she wore to those functions were conceived and fashioned in the small frame house of our Miss Evelyn. Needless to say, her talent was in great demand, and one must speak to her well in advance if she wished a certain frock for a special occasion. While waiting to be tried on in the lower room of her two room house with kitchen annex, the sounds of a country hoedown often came drifting down the narrow stairway. Jock was playing a fiddle. This accomplishment took precedence over being part time miller, for it resulted in occasional requests for playing at square dances in and about the village. A frail little woman, Miss Evelyn also found time to give a few beginners piano lessons. When passing her house, one often saw through the window a young pupil perched high on a stool before the upright piano. "One and two, and . . . " she would wave her hand, keeping time for hesitant small fingers.

A tiny building on the road at the far end of the village changed occupancy many times. I seem to remember it best as Miss Elsie's Millinery Shop. Miss Elsie carried straw and felt shapes in season, suited to all ages, from a little girl's Polk bonnet to a grownup's picture hat. There was an assortment of trimmings from which to

FINE FEATHERS

choose . . . satin and grosgrain ribbon, feathers and bright, artificial flowers. This gentle little woman had come to our small town from I don't know where, along with her brother who was recognized as being strange in manner and way. Indeed, tragedy touched our village one Saturday night when a shooting followed an altercation between this man and one of our colored citizens. Sharp in my picture memory is the sight of an ox cart moving at snail like pace down the dusty road in front of our yard. With a meaningful crack of his short cowhide whip, the driver mumbled terse commands such as "Haw" and "Gee" to his team of oxen as they plodded slowly on heavy feet, swinging their great yoked heads in unison. Stretched along the tongue of the cart was a crude coffin, and seated thereon the lamenting form of an old colored woman. Snatches of hymns, mumbled bits of prayer, and an occasional wail, broke the quiet of the summer's day. Aunt Betty Ann was accompanying her son's body for burial.

A VIRGINIA VILLAGE

6

THE ART OF LEARNING

To fill the important need of education, it was the custom for those on plantations or country estates to hire a tutor who lived in the home and participated in all social affairs, as well as everyday family life. In the small town or village, however, children were taught at home by some member of the family, or were taught in a private school composed of young members of several families under the tutelage of one teacher. Four families in our village engaged in such an endeavor, and we began our education in the little schoolhouse near our vegetable garden behind the hedge. In spring, the fragrance of early bloom and smell of newly plowed earth flowed in through the open windows as the garden was made ready for planting. There were sweet, tender young beets, heads of garden lettuce, early onions, rows of tiny peas. There was also a strawberry bed, along with fig and raspberry bushes, and near the back of the little school building, a heavy grape arbor. Inside we each had a slant top desk with groove for pencils. There was a blackboard on an easel and my grandmother's big square piano with yellowed ivory keys. School opened each morning with saying The Lord's Prayer and singing the National Anthem, followed by simple ballads and hymns accompanied by the tinny old piano: "Flow Gently, Sweet Afton," "Annie Laurie," "Onward Christian Soldiers," etc.

Once there came a time when we were facing the school year without a teacher, and it was then that our parents and three neighboring families advertised in The Southern Churchman for "A Young Christian Lady of Culture and Refinement." This, then, was how it came about that Miss Frances Cox arrived that fall to instill guidance and learning in our little group. The haze of autumn hung over woods and field, and goldenrod lighted the dusty roadside on the morning that two of the fathers set out to meet the steamboat. It was with high spirits that they awaited the young woman who would bring in a breath of fresh air to the stagnant little village. In such a mood they waited for the boat to be unloaded, casually watching the stevedores trundle one-wheel carts of freight from the vessel's hold. They glanced disinterestedly at a lone old woman on the far deck, and wondered aloud would their passenger be a fragile blonde, sultry brunette, or fiery redhead. Any moment now she would appear, and they kept bright smiles of welcome. Moments passed, and the last bit of freight deposited, still no one came. What if she had missed the boat, they wondered with sagging smiles. Had she become ill? What if they had mistaken the time of her arrival? What if (an impossible thought) the old woman on the deck . . . could she be? She could.

Feeling her way down the gangplank with the aid of a black, cotton umbrella, the homely old woman peered blindly from behind steel-rimmed spectacles, her long, sallow face exaggerated by a mammoth chin where a large mole grew several wispy whiskers. From her voluminous black skirt to the wide brim hat adorned with a pair of stiff bird wings, she was pathetically dreary. The cause was completely lost when later she faced her young charges who soon learned she was partially deaf as well as near sighted. They soon got the upper hand. Our distraught teacher had just one ally, my sister, who felt a compassion for the old soul and occasionally took her riding in the topless buggy, pulled by the old mare, "Hattie." I can still see the little girl, her black curls blowing in the wind, the old lady sitting erect beside her on the high seat, holding aloft the black umbrella over the winged hat.

Each day Miss Cox set aside a special time to take what she called "a little recess" when she would depart for the garden behind the school. Inevitably there came a day when her young students crowded to the back window to see what was of interest to their teacher in the dormant grape arbor. Wide eyed, they saw her lift the hem of her black serge skirt and, from a small pocket in her taffeta petticoat, remove a small bag. Dipping in thumb and forefinger, she adroitly held a pinch of powder to each nostril. Miss Cox took snuff! Unhappily, the old soul did not meet requirements, and her tenure in the little school behind the hedge was of brief duration.

The public schools established in county seats offered little opportunity for children restricted by limited transportation over muddy dirt roads, and it was the one room school that continued to fill an important need in the back country for grades one through seven. Unlike the little red schoolhouse of picture book fame, the small, one room buildings were crude and uninviting, with the barest of essentials. One year a young man in our village became the sole teacher in such a school in a remote settlement some miles from the village. It was a buggy and horse that provided the surest transportation during snowy winter months. The following summer some of us were invited to the closing exercises. So, on a bright June morning we crowded into a Model T for our first and last visit to a one room school. Sunlight flickered through overhead leaves in a wooded portion of the road, casting blobs of yellow on the loamy earth, rutted by narrow buggy rims and an occasional tire track.

A VIRGINIA VILLAGE

In a clearing at the road's end stood the small, unpainted building—forlorn, desolate, isolated, supported in its isolation by a leaning outside privy and dejected well. Inside it was Spartan in its simplicity, with the whitewashed walls and hard wooden benches, where we were given seats alongside parents and other guests. Following some last minute instructions, the program began. A freckle faced little girl with tight braided pigtails and lively blue eyes offered her best. Her flowered cotton dress hung limply about her thin body—the dipping hemline meeting at times her high button shoes.

> Down in the meadow in the grass and the sun
> Lived an old mother frog, and her little frog one.
> 'Croak,' said the mother; 'I croak,' said the one,
> And it croaked and it croaked in the grass and the sun.
>
> Down in the meadow where the stream runs blue
> Lived an old mother fish and her little fishes two.
> 'Swim,' said the mother; 'We swim,' said the two,
> And they swam and they swam where the stream runs blue.

On and on she recited the many verses of the familiar little poem in her singsong treble. There were other recitations and a spelling bee, the children cutting up and down in the line, the winner receiving a coveted prize. There were other things I remember, but the memory that remains outstanding was the singing. Lined against the wall, the entire group—from lisping first graders to self-conscious teens—sang in unison. There were well-scrubbed boys, with tanned bare feet beneath faded overalls, hair slicked back from sunburned forehead, girls with shoes and without, proudly conscious of a best-printed cotton or voile of uncertain size. Faces alive with happiness and achievement, they sang unrestrained the hit tunes of the day . . . "Yes Sir, That's My Baby," "Nobody Lied," "They Got Hot Lips,"

THE ART OF LEARNING

"Running Wild, Lost Control" . . . modern jazz, taught them by their young teacher with the help of a wind-up victrola. Words and music they did not understand from a segment of life they had never known. It was indeed incongruous. It could have been amusing had there not been an element of pathos.

How much factual knowledge, how much textbook learning they had acquired, I do not know. But it is safe to say a handful of children "off the beaten track" had their year made brighter by a young man who brought the lighter things he was familiar with into their lives of bare essentials. A freezer of homemade ice cream, packed beneath a double thickness of grass sacks, completed their happiness, and brought to an end the school year.

A VIRGINIA VILLAGE

7
PICTURE MEMORIES

Should one form in his mind some picture of a village, it might evoke a postcard image in bright colors: a white house in a cluster of green trees beside a yellow road and, silhouetted above the roof tops, the spire of a little church. Perhaps it would be a winter scene of snow, with bare tree limbs etched against a setting sun, a spiral of gray smoke rising from a red chimney. Having been born and bred in such surroundings, it is natural my mind's picture centers upon the village with which I am most familiar, the village of my birth and early childhood. It was in no manner a postcard village. It was in no sense picturesque. It was not particularly appealing to anyone just passing through. Rather, its charm lay in its wholesome atmosphere, its very special people.

Living in rural surroundings, small things unnoticed in a more sophisticated place become of great importance. There are moments so fleeting, happenings so trivial, they are seemingly not worth recording, but they depict a way of life. This is especially true of children on whose uncluttered mind things come into clear focus. Free of outside distractions, they are drawn close to nature.

Have you ever searched the woods in spring for tiny fragrant arbutus, gathered ferns beneath the boughs of a lofty pine, or found a stray hickory nut in your path? Have you ever searched for a four leaf clover, or found the fragile shell of a locust shed on the bark of a tree? Did you hold the golden dust of a buttercup against your chin to see if you like butter, or pluck the petals from a daisy to tell your fortune? Did you fish for gray spiders through a small hole in the ground with the stem of a wild onion, or tell the time with a spent dandelion? Have you watched a soft cocoon hanging low from a branch, or caught a grasshopper and chanted, "Grasshopper, grasshopper, give

A VIRGINIA VILLAGE

me some 'lassies and I'll turn you loose?" ("Lassies" was a sticky substance exuded by the frightened grasshopper, which reminded us of molasses.) Did you form pictures from the shape of the clouds as you lay faceup on the grass or, facedown, watch tiny ants about their sand hill? Have you captured lightening bugs in a bottle, tied a string to the leg of a June bug, or stood on tiptoe to see a robin's nest? Did you make a wish upon a falling star, look at a new moon over your left shoulder for luck, press a wildflower for keeping between the pages of a book? Did you make a visit to the country store to choose your first Valentine of a red heart with skirt of paper lace and sentimental verse? All these simple things are woven into the life of the child growing up in the country.

Inspired by the nature poems of Jean Ingelow, at twelve I composed the following:

BLYTHE BIRD

    Sing Blythe Bird in the old tree top
      Where apple blooms cluster and sway.
    Sing and be happy, for springtime is here
      And the sun shines brightly today.

    What is it you're so merry oe'r
      As on the green bough you swing?
    Is it the world so full of joy
      That you those tidings must bring?

    Is it that your pretty mate dwells
      Up where the leaves are green?
    Could it be your little ones sleep
      Safe in their nest in between?

PICTURE MEMORIES

I know your wee nestlings there
    Are hushed to sleep every night
By a low singing wind rocking their bed
    Till they open bright eyes to the light.

DAWN

Dawn now breaks in the rosy East
    Turning the night to day;
God has sent the light again
    To guide us on our way.

Its golden rays reach down and touch
    The housetops, fields and lake;
Flowers slowly unfold their buds
    Birds begin to awake.

Grass is sparkling with diamond dew
    That fell in the velvet night;
A little buttercup's petals are full
    As it holds them up to the light.

The dandelion lifts its soft green stem
    From the warmth of its loamy bed;
The cool west wind bows down to earth
    And kisses its gold topped head.

A VIRGINIA VILLAGE

8
IPECAC AND THINGS

Everyone knew him as "Doctor" or "Doc." They said he was especially good in cases of pneumonia and had pulled many a one through with his famous mustard plasters—a homemade remedy comprising a piece of cloth spread with a paste consisting of a beaten white of egg mixed with mustard, covered with tissue paper. After applying to the patient this "counter irritant" (as he called it), the doctor, nurse and friend would sit by the bedside until the crisis had passed. In the opinion of the neighborhood, this proficiency was excelled only by his skill in delivering babies. In this he had surely "missed his calling." The rural countryside was populated with many generations the doctor had given a start in life. He "saw them through" from a few drops of ipecac to a croupy baby, and the ensuing childhood diseases, on into adulthood.

I can remember him when he would enter the nursery to "tend" one of us sick children. Clean shaven and pink cheeked, the doctor brought with him into the sick room a faint odor of talcum powder and Bay Rum, subordinated to the indescribable smell of medicine when he opened his black satchel. In retrospect this seems to have been a composite of creosote camphor, wintergreen, and the pungent smell of tannic bark. There were no "wonder drugs" in those days, and the homely remedies prescribed are as out of date as the doctor's stiff collar and the gold watch fob that hung from his vest pocket.

The examination always began with the request to "stick out your tongue," and it was from this observation the good doctor informed himself as to how to prescribe. It was common in this low country to be given to "bilious attacks," and the dosage was the inevitable calomel, followed by the dreaded castor oil. The little pink pills were carefully counted and left on the starched, white bureau scarf. The castor oil, always on hand, sat just inside the physic press, an omen of what might befall you. Recommending a little egg albumen or, better still, a milk toddy for nourishment, the physician would close his black bag, give the patient an affectionate pat on the head and settle back for a brief social visit.

The doctor was an unforgettable blend of adult and child, with a high nasal voice and ruddy complexion. Fastidious in his dress, his blue suit was neatly pressed and his high, white collar spotless above his jaunty necktie. Indeed, one of the first times I remember seeing my mother lose her patience was once when a child was sick and my father had been dispatched in the night for the doctor. Though his home was only a few doors away, the minutes slipped into the better part of an hour before he came. "For Heaven's sake, Doctor, what took you so long?" my mother exclaimed. His white shirt was neatly buttoned, his tie carefully arranged with the familiar stickpin, and his hair brushed to its accustomed smoothness.

This was the day when the automobile was fast supplanting the horse and carriage. For many years, the doctor's high-topped buggy was a familiar sight on the winding country roads on his errands of mercy. Late at night, it was often his faithful mare, "Nelly," who found their way home . . . the doctor asleep over the reins. Long used to this means of transportation, he never really mastered the automobile. Once he drove with undue speed into his own lane, and as he reared back on the wheel of his Model T, was heard to shout, "Whoa, Nelly." Once, they say, he turned across the highway near his drug store in front of an oncoming, out-of-state car, with the inevitable crash and crumpling of fenders. The old "Doc" alighted and, facing the irate stranger, admonished

IPECAC AND THINGS

him in his inimitable way: "Man, you should have known I was going to turn into my drug store."

There were many amusing stories that gave a true insight into the personality of the old physician. He was a willing companion for a day of fishing, and could "hold his own," as he put it, with the boys in the back room when "sitting in" on a game of poker. Known for his amiable disposition, he was also known for being tight with a dollar. One day, two young men from the village entered his drug store where he was sitting, as usual, behind the counter at a vantage spot. There he could greet friends and also lend an ear to the clang of the cash register. "Boys," he said, "how

about some beer? The treat's on me." "This is mighty nice of you, Doc," said Alex, unbelievingly. "Yes, its mighty nice," responded Frank with the same reaction, as they followed him into the back room that served as the doctor's office. "Sit down, boys." He pulled forward two straight chairs and, going to the door, called to the clerk up front, "Oh, Ruth, bring back a bottle of beer and three glasses."

A VIRGINIA VILLAGE

The back office is indelibly printed upon my memory. A small room, it contained a high, oblong table, holding some dusty medical books and a collection of outdated magazines. Upon a stained green blotter, bearing the name of a local insurance company, was an overflowing ashtray, and the familiar three-monkey paperweight. Two straight wooden chairs accompanied a Morris Chair with faded upholstery and sagging springs. Lee and his generals looked down from a sidewall, and nearby, slightly askew, the doctor's framed license proclaimed his right to practice medicine. Most prominently displayed was his prized possession, a lithograph of four dogs playing poker—a collie, a bulldog, a setter and a small dog of uncertain origin, holding in their paws some cards. Pointing to the last mentioned canine, the doctor declared with a child-like delight, "You can almost tell what he's got in his hand by his expression."

Sunday evening was set aside for his weekly social visit to our house, at which time he and my father would rehash old news, discuss current politics, with a final review of the stock market. One evening the doctor arrived, looked especially pleased, and seating himself in his usual chair, brightly proclaimed, "Judge, I figured the best way to beat the stock market." "Well now, Doc," my father replied, curiously amused, "That's worth hearing." "I don't know why I have not thought of it before," came the naive reply. "It's this simple: you just buy them when they are low and sell them when they're high."

Many years passed and with them both of my parents. We five children, now grown, were scattered in various places. I, known to the old doctor as "Sal Jane," had recently married and returned to the village to live, when the inevitable misunderstanding between newly-weds arose. Petulant and spoiled, I sought consolation from my old friend and tie to the past. I called the old doctor and asked him to come to see me. Turning to him for sympathy and perhaps advice, I was careful not to give a specific complaint. Already I felt comforted on hearing the high-pitched familiar voice say, "I'll be right up, Sal Jane." With age added to his customary slowness, time elapsed during which the misunderstanding was smoothed over. I secretly wondered when I heard his step on the porch what reason to give him for my urgent call. My apprehension was unfounded. He arrived with his customary warm greeting. Making himself comfortable for a social visit, he not once inquired as to my well being.

From a few drops of ipecac to a croupy baby to the more complex behavior of an adult, he was ripe in the wisdom of years. Physician, neighbor, friend, he had come that night without the familiar black bag.

A VIRGINIA VILLAGE

9

BEGINNINGS

Along with the addition of a drug store in the village was added the important telephone office, commonly known as "Central," housed in one room and presided over by a single operator, known affectionately as Lizzie. During the years when I was away at boarding school, it was Lizzie who ably filled me in as to the whereabouts of my parents when and if our phone did not answer. "Deed, they are some place about the village," she advised. "I'm sure it was just this morning your mother called Ike Hall's store for bacon and sugar. Fact is," she added, "it hasn't been long when I saw her and your father drive by."

Before this means of communication through Lizzie and the Central Office, no calls beyond the confines of the village were possible. I recall our first telephone hung on the kitchen wall: an ugly wooden box like thing, with two metal ovals above the mouthpiece, as eyes above a nose. The receiver hung on a black cord to the left, a small handle for ringing on the right. A turn of the handle would get you Cousin John, who could connect you with local calls from a room behind the post office. He also ran the post office. Indeed, neither occupation seemed really suited, for his limp brown moustache and trustful brown eyes behind horn rimmed glasses suggested more a shy professor.

It was a well known fact that Cousin John raised a fine vegetable garden back of his gray frame house, and he also raised flowers of the common garden variety: spicy nasturtiums, bright marigolds, sweet Williams and hardy zinnias, in most colors of the rainbow. But, it was the sunflowers that were his special pride, for some said they were "fit to take a prize, they were that tall." Most especially, Cousin John was thought of for his accommodating ways. It was said he would "trot his legs off" to take a message or deliver a bundle, "he was that accommodating." Whenever there was any small job of some importance that no one else had time for, one thought of Cousin John.

Later each home and place of business in the village had its special ring, like two shorts, one long, two longs and a short. This important advancement allowed us to call directly to those about the village, or even within a radius of a few miles out from the village. It stands to reason that everyone tried out this exciting new addition; that is, all but Mama, who said she "simply did not trust the thing." After days of persuasion, Mama finally agreed to use the phone. Hesitatingly, she asked Cousin John to "get me Sunnyside," the farm where my grandmother lived outside of the village. "Hello, Hello! Is that you, Josie? This is Sally. I am talking on the telephone." After a pause, "I declare, it's as if you were here in this very room. Indeed, it is downright frightening . . . I'm not sure I like it." She impulsively dropped the receiver, leaving it dangling on its long cord. "Now," she stated firmly to all of us surrounding her, "Now, I have done it. I have talked." There was a note of finality to her voice, and it was some time before she would touch the thing again. But this was a time of change, of improvements and additions, and soon we could talk to places at a distance by placing the call through the switchboard.

One thing seemed to follow another, and now a sensational new invention that would revolutionize the nation was sweeping the country. It was the talk of everyone, this horseless buggy, this mechanical vehicle called an automobile. In our village, the first one was bought by Mr. Willie Wallace, who was the proprietor and owner of the modest little hotel. With admiration and curiosity, tinged with a bit of envy, it was examined and profoundly dis-

BEGINNINGS

cussed under the proud supervision of the owner. Very soon after, as I recall, Papa casually announced to the family that Willie Wallace had taken him for a ride in his new automobile. This astonishing news we received with excited enthusiasm, and we looked at Papa with respect and awe. But Mama heartily disapproved of taking such a chance! "Why, no one could know just what the monstrous machine might do," seemingly referring to it as if it had a mind and will of its own. But, nevertheless, it was the day Papa took a drive with Mr. Wallace he was bitten by the proverbial bug.

Just as there was our first telephone, so there was also our first automobile. It was a touring car, with curtains to snap on in bad weather—a forerunner of the glassed-in sedan. It was a memorable day, a red letter day, when the affable and pompous dealer delivered our first car, with leather upholstery and shiny nickel, to the front gate. After some instructions from the knowledgeable agent, Papa declared he was ready to handle it alone, choosing the backfield to demonstrate his ability. Many in our part of the little town, drawn to the sight of the shining car that stopped at our gate, were attracted also to the unparalleled happening about to take place behind the barn. Wide-eyed, excited, proud, we children were admonished to stay well behind the protective barnyard fence. Round and round the field Papa drove, hands clasped firmly on the wheel, eyes fixed straight ahead, as the frightened cattle, their tails held high, scattered wildly in every direction. Papa appeared very calm and nonchalant as he continued to circle. I wondered how many circles he would take to prove he could "handle things" alone. Finally, on one of the bouts, "How do you stop it?" he called out to the agent on the edge of the field. Ensconced behind a gatepost, Mama, alarm added to her already dubious confidence, called, "Get out of that thing, Joe. Get out at once. Get out before you are killed." Papa couldn't get out. "Turn off the switch key," the dealer shouted. Slowly, the car coasted to a stop and Papa got out. "It would have eventually run out of gas," Papa said.

Unbelievably, after so short a time, Papa decided to take the family on their first trip in our car. Totally oblivious to circuitous country roads of an unimproved nature, we were to drive to Newport News to visit my grandmother, a rambling trip in that day of some 200 miles. Mama, after being driven several times to the nearby grocery store, had become reconciled to the "monstrous machine." Happily, she took her seat up front, my little sister on her lap, and the

other four of us children arranged on the spacious back seat. In the trunk, or boot, there was an inviting picnic basket of lunch, along with sleeping attire and a change of clothes all around for tomorrow. Hardly had we gone a distance of twenty miles when both boys were overcome with pangs of hunger, insisting that we eat right then. It seemed that no one else was averse to the idea, so lunch was spread on a high table in a country churchyard.

BEGINNINGS

It proved a long, hot journey, much of it over little-traveled back roads bordered by thick wooded areas. Oft as not, we were mired down in heavy sand or muddy holes, and my brothers would assist Papa in combing the roadsides for branches to place under the spinning tires. My small sister and I took advantage of such opportunities to shed our shoes and socks, stretch our legs, and ease our bare feet in the cool mud. Late evening, we arrived at our destination, four pairs of dirty, bare feet hanging over the sides of the automobile. We must preserve the shiny new leather of the interior.

It was a wondrous sight, my first sight of a city, such as it was. Endless pavements bordered small front yards where houses lay close together. Flickering gas lamps lighted occasional street corners. I noticed there were no big yards for setting up a game of croquet, and no trees to hide behind when playing "I spy"—both a decided disadvantage.

It was like a fairy tale when I went with my grandmother the next morning to visit stores, their big glass fronts holding life-size dolls dressed like grown-ups. It was a baby doll in sweater and cap that swelled my heart with love and longing. I stood with my nose pressed against the glass in admiration. I wanted to take it home. I could not have this window display. I cried.

It was nice to get back home to our big yard and familiar playmates. I would not trade my village for all the cities in the whole wide world.

I think you could count the following "a first," because there had never been anything like it to occur in our little village. It all came about when a prominent statesman, who lived there, died, and the whole community became involved to some extent. He had obtained independence for a Pacific island people, and they, in appreciation, sent a large delegation to his funeral at our small country church. The village people opened their hearts and homes to a throng of outsiders, including dignitaries from our nation's capitol and elsewhere, and people from the distant Pacific island. Our next door neighbor, a relative of the deceased, acted as hostess in her home on that day, welcoming those from a distance in her own gracious way. Afterwards, she told the following story on herself. Noticing a distinguished, well-dressed gentleman, seemingly alone and apparently very distressed, she concluded he must surely be a very close relative or friend of the deceased. Approaching, she introduced herself, adding graciously, "Thank you so much for coming. Cousin Willie would be so pleased to know you are here." She learned later he was the funeral director.

It was, of course, a great tribute to our distinguished citizen when the island people gave a large mausoleum in his memory. It was, however, a source of much concern to the people of the community where to place a monument of such large proportions and unique design, constructed of varied colored marble and granite. In all truth, it was not in keeping with the conservative taste of our village, and no place seemed just right for the ponderous edifice, which finally came to rest in our simple churchyard.

The mausoleum was enclosed on two sides by low walls of granite and marble. To the back, the figure of an island girl offered up a wreath of flowers to the white marble bust of the deceased. Above the bust hovered the American eagle. At the dedication ceremony, when the veil was pulled from the shining marble likeness, an old black man on the fringe of the crowd was heard to exclaim, "Lawd A'mighty, dat buzzard gonna git dat old man for sure." Where else but in this small village would such a work of art evoke such a comment?

10

A BIT OF ENGLAND

How fortunate we were to have many relatives living close by, relatives who each in his or her own special way enriched our lives, and whom I remember today with nostalgia and affection.

As the high back buggy and slow gait of "Old Branch," the horse, neared our lane, we knew Aunt Fanny was coming. Aunt Fanny lived a few miles out from the village on a farm called "The Glebe," where a spreading pecan tree in the front yard supplied abundance of nuts in fall, bountiful shade in summer. From a low limb, a fringed hammock was a popular refuge on a hot day and, nearby, the home post and double wickets marked the beginning of a croquet ground. In the shade of the old tree we would cut fat striped watermelons, previously lowered into the well for cooling. Sitting around on the ground, we children gouged out the sweet red meat to the last blush of pink. To go deeper would give one "fits," or such was old wives' tale.

The homemade table and chairs beneath the protective boughs of the big tree at The Glebe proved a convenient place for "putting up" fruits and vegetables from nearby orchard and garden. Aunt Fanny, in checked gingham apron, patiently peeled fuzzy skins from rough cheeks of peaches, dropping smooth halves into glass jars. A brandied peach is surely the most delicious use made of this fruit. During the First World War, when brandy was hard to obtain, it was found that burying the jars underground with sugar and alcohol resulted, after so long a time, in almost a facsimile.

To make wine, grapes and sugar were set aside to ferment in large crocks in the basement. Twice during the fermenting time, if my memory serves me right, the thick foam was skimmed from the top, the liquid strained through cheesecloth. Then a final straining, and the clear red wine was ready for bottling. It took its place in the cellar lock-room, along with jars of transparent jelly under white paraffin caps.

The Glebe, a typical farmhouse, was usually in a state of confused disorder excepting, perhaps, the parlor, with its stiff, over-stuffed furniture. Upon a crocheted mat on the parlor table, a bulging oil lamp was decorated on bowl and globe with a full-blown rose. Mid-center the mantle reposed a narrow upright clock, its small dial lost in a labyrinth of brass scroll above a beguiling Cupid. Jardinieres of fern and Wandering Jew sat on tripod stands by the windows.

I can now feel the warmth of the sunny kitchen, its windows aglow with red geraniums, a gray cat asleep on the wood box in

A BIT OF ENGLAND

the corner. I can almost taste the cool, fresh buttermilk from the stone churn with fleur-de-lis on the side and long-handled wooden splatter. I remember the worn pine table and the Blue Willow plates standing on their rims in the cupboard.

Most especially, I remember Aunt Fanny. Dear Aunt Fanny, with her blue eyes, gnarled hands, and white bun high on her head. Simple and gentle, she was truly a child at heart. It was Aunt Fanny we begged for when recovering from some childhood sickness. The way I think of her most is in fresh calico shirtwaist, a gold breast pin with a lock of hair in the casing, her floor-length black skirt molding her plump hips, and the familiar wicker basket over her arm. The brown wicker basket with lid tightly closed usually held a surprise for the sick one. It could be a cup of golden custard or a square of gingerbread. Once there was a live squab from her own barn loft. The best of all, however, was when she pulled her chair close to the sick bed and, from an apron pocket, removed her crocheting. Then, with glasses perched low on her nose, she told for the hundredth time of when she was a little girl in England.

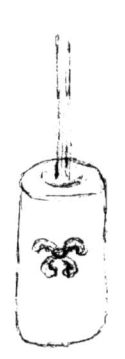

It could have been a fairy tale, it was that fantastic. She, having lived in that faraway country, played with children of another world. One could almost see the rolling green countryside, smell the Hawthorne hedges, and hear the laughter of children playing hopscotch on the sidewalks. It was a fabulous story of which we never tired: her visits to the Wax Museum, the Old Crystal Palace, Westminster Abbey, all these places and things which were a part of her life in the Old Country. My grandfather, then a Consul to

A VIRGINIA VILLAGE

England, had of course taken his family with him, including my mother, who was at that time about six years old.

The children had acquired in England a little yellow canary bird named "Doc" that they attempted to bring home with them after their time overseas drew to a close. On that rough winter's crossing, with every swell of the sea, Doc's cage, hanging high in the hold of the ship, would swing wildly, and the little bird sing happily. Daily trips were made below to feed the small passenger, and Doc became known to all on board. At sea on Christmas day, the ship's cook baked a large fruitcake for the voyagers in honor of the season. This was thought to have caused the death of the canary, for some well-meaning friend had fed it a crumb of the cake and it died, perhaps from acute indigestion—or so my grandfather thought. Even the drop of brandy he administered failed to revive it.

In talking about Aunt Fanny, it seems befitting I speak of Mr. Constable, her husband. He was a small, blustering Englishman with a white beard, bright blue eyes and a limp from an old injury. I never really knew how he found his way to Virginia where he met and married my Aunt Fanny, settling down on a farm. Soon his weathered face and homespun attire bespoke a man of the soil. One would not guess the rough hands could guide the smallest paintbrushes in fashioning delicate flower or landscape.

For some winters following Mr. Constable's death, Aunt Fanny moved into the village for the winter months to escape the hardships of the farm. She drove back to the farm most every day, however, to "see how things were going," and to speak to the hired man who tended the stock. One day in fall she asked my brother and me if we would like to drive there with her. We climbed happily and eagerly into the old buggy and squeezed against plump Aunt Fanny on the narrow seat. Aunt Fanny made a "cluck" with her tongue and Old Branch, with a disdainful switch of her tail, was off with a slow clop. There were several interesting things about the buggy to talk about on the way, such as the high spatter-board to protect one's bare knees. On the driver's side was a narrow pouch for holding a buggy whip—in this instance, empty. The buggy contained on the back end a small box-like place for keeping things. I wondered what Aunt Fanny had there in the brown sack. I wished it might be apples. "You can, if you like," she said on getting there, "pick up some chips on the woodpile and put them in that slatted basket. But never mind," she added, "you might find something you would rather do." So saying, she drove off down a back farm road in search of the tenant.

There were many things to see . . . to explore: the silo, the milk house, the big farm bell used to summon the men from the fields for midday dinner. There was also the cavernous old barn with cupola on top where pigeons made soft, throaty sounds as they flew in and out. The time passed, and all at once the silence of the closed house, the stillness of the surroundings, penetrated our play. There was not even the security of seeing horse and buggy tied nearby, a sure proof that Aunt Fanny was somewhere around. She had been gone too long . . . much too long. A few more chips in the slatted basket, then a few more. We decided she had forgotten us and gone home. We must leave, too. "Do you know the way?" I asked my brother, my heart pounding. "Sure," he said with manly authority, "Come on." We started running down the long lane bordered by heavy woods. "What about bears?" I said, glancing into the forest of trees. "Shucks, I am not afraid. Besides, there are no bears." Though he was younger than I, I depended on his knowledge and protection. It seemed hours before we reached the boundaries of the village and familiar places. Only then could we slow down to a walk.

A VIRGINIA VILLAGE

"Does your mother know where you are?" It was the nice editor of our paper in the door of his printing shop. Our dirty faces (mine streaked with tears) were enough to lend suspicion, for we were never allowed to go to the village alone. He phoned our mother to let her know we were on our way home for she might be worried. Such was this example of kindness and concern manifested by friends in our village. The white fence around our yard became a boundary for the following week, punishment for running away from The Glebe.

Poor Aunt Fanny, she must have been dreadfully upset not finding us when she returned from the backfield. "I even looked down the well," she told my mother as she tied the old horse to the gatepost in our lane.

11
DIFFERENT PEOPLE

Almost daily she was seen about the village, the haughty old lady, walking with a springy step and erect carriage. Having spent most of her life elsewhere in the field of education, she had returned to the village to make her home in a small cottage she called "The Wren's Nest." A profusion of bloom in the side yard bespoke her love for flowers, which, in turn, bespoke a softer image beneath her stern exterior. She had never married—the homely old lady with prominent nose and slate colored eyes behind pince nez glasses. Her lined and weathered face might be attributed to age, but more likely it was exposure to the elements. For many years she had lived and taught in a mountainous section of Virginia where, partly through necessity and partly through choice, she walked in all weather. It was said she thought nothing of braving sub zero temperatures for extended hikes in the foothills. Disciplined, Spartan in her way of life, she would frequently enjoy a game of cards. In the past, her chosen sport was riding horseback sidesaddle in divided skirt, sitting as stiffly erect as a commander. In her late life when she disapproved, the formidable old lady had a way of clicking her dentures and shaking her head in agitation, the glasses trembling on her prominent nose. One would think this austere old soul, with her rigid rules and intolerance, would have been feared and disliked by her students. She was, but the memory of her mellowed with time. Her students came to realize the benefits of her teaching, which had been drummed into their unwilling ears. They even wrote and told her so, and it was very gratifying. She did not have many close friends. In spite of her excellent mind, her years of success as a teacher, her seeming self-reliance, and the flowers blooming in her side yard, she was really lonely.

Only by staying a while in our village could one be aware of all the inhabitants, for there were some rarely seen and seldom spoken of. An outsider, a casual visitor, would not know the four stout middle-aged sisters in their small cottage on the far side of the village. The eldest took in light sewing—mending that is—and the youngest, the most sprightly, had a position of some worth in the back room of the newspaper office. There was the one everybody was especially fond of, the one with gentle ways and quiet manners, a practical nurse whose capable presence in a sickroom endeared her to all who knew her. Finally, one must not forget the fourth sister, the pretty one with classic features and a creamy complexion—the one who was the most obese, with a gawky, uncoordinated body. Fidgety and frequently thick of tongue, her brow was constantly moist, and small beads of perspiration fringed her top lip. Often she was seen miles out of the village, walking with quick, agile steps in spite of her unwieldy body. Kindly, mild of manner, she must have made a strange impression on those who did not know her. Those of the village did, and understood.

Everyone liked him, the friendly village barber, and through the door of his small shop both young and old came from all about. They came to get a haircut, they came seeking companionship and to hear the latest news and the latest gossip. The small shop was, in all truth, their club of sorts. There were usually others in the smoke-filled room, with seats tilted against the wall. The barber, slight of build, his black hair slicked back from his pale forehead, wore a rakish bow tie and boldly plaid pants. His overall appearance suggested a flamboyancy that belied his quiet manner and conservative ways. It was a love of hunting dogs that was his

DIFFERENT PEOPLE

hobby, and the calendar above the barber's chair usually depicted a pair of keen pointers or English Setters . . . perhaps a covey of quail flushing from the underbrush. "'Twas a crying shame," they all exclaimed when once he was cited for contempt of court. It was not a grave offense. He just "plumb forgot" he had been summoned to jury duty. It was that simple. A light sentence was imposed of a few days in the little brick jail. Some friends brought a rug for the bare brick floor. Others brought a reading lamp, along with some magazines. Yet another brought a home-cooked dinner to be replaced on the morrow. His absence from the small shop where the red and white pole turned six days a week created something just short of a controversy. Where was one to get his hair cut, to say nothing of the loss of his warm companionship? There was such a general hue and cry that the light sentence was modified by the powers that be. Now the red and white pole would continue to turn by day, and the well-liked barber was given the keys to the small brick jail so that he might return the next few nights to the plain little room with its special rug and reading lamp to lend a friendly warmth.

Having once seen her, she was not easily forgotten, the old colored woman who caused heads to turn in obvious curiosity. It mattered not what the weather; her short, dumpy figure was grotesque under an extraordinary assortment of clothes, as she made her way to the crossroads store on a back country road. Her unique apparel consisted of sweaters of different colors, sizes and weights, worn over a calico skirt and topped by a hip-length jacket. Layers of different hemlines denoted a variety of skirts of varied weight and texture beneath a blue-checked apron. Swinging loosely over all, a man's overcoat hung to her feet, which were wrapped in a flower-type carpeting. As if this was not enough, a fringed shawl draped her shoulders, and the white cloth tied about her head contrasted with her small, brown face. To top off this spectacle, there were several layers of hats, one upon the other, of many shapes and kinds. She shuffled happily along with the aid of a hickory stick, her head wreathed in the smoke from her corncob pipe. As vividly as I remember the odd appearance of the old woman in her heterogeneous assortment of clothes, it is the memory of her pert little nod, the gay salute of her small brown hand, which stays with me.

12

BOUNTY

Perhaps we did not have what might be called exotic or fancy menus, for it was not our way. In all truth, we preferred the well tried recipes of old cook books from our own kitchens, or carefully preserved family recipes, handed down from generation to generation. Blessed with an abundance of nature's finest gifts from both land and water, it seemed our one lack was fresh fruits and vegetables during winter months. This was before the day when the chain stores and supermarkets with their oversized trucks and refrigerated vans found their way to remote villages. Some fifty miles from a railroad, we were dependent upon the steamboats for shipments in and out, but then they had no refrigeration for keeping perishables. It stands to reason that those things not native to this area were hard to come by, and an orange in the toe of a Christmas stocking was an exceptional and welcomed treat.

There was all manner of seafood in the Tidewater section, enough to supply local needs with plenty left over. At least once a week the fisherman came to our doors, bringing his catch fresh from the waters in and about "The Neck," as they called it. This consisted of whatever species were "running" at the time. Rockfish, rich Blues, millpond Bass, the very exceptional Shad, and somewhere in the big fish box on the wagon or truck was usually a string of catfish. Not to be overlooked were delicious, small butter fish, spot, and perch delivered from the watermen's seines, and from countless crab pots came those shellfish to add much to local tables. Last but not least, there were Tidewater's famous oysters, to suit the taste and fancy.

A VIRGINIA VILLAGE

With the woods, fields and brush teeming with wild life, it was truly a "hunter's paradise": wild duck to be shot over frozen ponds, quail to be hunted in the open fields, and the small rail bird, or sora, to take from swaying marshes. There were rabbits and squirrels in the shelter of woods, and frogs to "gig" in the still ponds. What with so much game, old cook books contained many recipes for preparing it. Some stipulate to filet a duck, while others call for splitting it down the back and baking. Still another called for cutting the bird in sections, covering it with stewed tomatoes, mushrooms, wine, and condiments of one kind or another, then cooking it inside the oven in a covered pan. My mother chose always to roast a duck, for she believed the simple way was the best way for retaining the delicate flavor of a Canvas Back or a Mallard. To the best of my recollection, the following was the way it was done:

WILD DUCK

Rub the fowl well with butter, both inside and out. Season with salt and stuff with a good breadcrumb dressing. Place in hot oven in a covered roasting pan with a small amount of water, as you would roast a hen. Baste frequently with wine. Orange juice is a substitute. A third choice is pickle juice. Cook well done, or when pricked with a fork, no blood oozes. Remove cover and brown. Cook less time if preferred not well done.

DRESSING FOR WILD DUCK

Crumble breadcrumbs (not too fine). Stale bread preferred. Amount needed for average size duck, about two cups. Dice celery and onion and add to crumbs. Add a dash of celery

BOUNTY

seed, salt, pepper and some bacon drippings, if available. Let stand some hours, if possible, to blend. Moisten with Cointreau to hold dressing together. Keep on dry side. If Cointreau is not available, use orange juice. Stuff duck.

QUAIL

Split the quail down the back, season with salt and pepper. Place breast down in skillet on top of stove with deep fat or grease. Cover with lid and weight down with one or more flat irons, or the equivalent. Remove lid for turning several times. Do not over cook.

With the many things commonly raised on a country place, there was small chance of a completely bare cupboard. Along with fresh milk, homemade butter and smooth brown eggs, there were fresh fruits and vegetables in season. Storerooms contained barrels of water-ground meal and flour, along with tins of lard. In addition to chicken, turkey, and perhaps guinea or some other domestic fowl, there was tender, young lamb. From rafters in the meat house hung smoked cured hams and shoulders, with slabs of middling or bacon salted away in a big box below. I am reminded of the words of an old country tune, parts of which went like this:

> Hambones am meat. Bacon am sweet.
> Possum meat am berry, berry fine.
> But give me, oh give me,
> I really wish you would,
> That watermillion smilin' on the vine.

I have heard vendors harking their wares on city streets, their familiar cries sounding through the neighborhood: "Watermillions

A VIRGINIA VILLAGE

. . . Ripe, cold, watermillions;" or "Strawberries . . . nice, ripe, strawberries." Such a colorful form of merchandising has disappeared, along with the ragman and his chant, "Here's yo ole ragman," and the sound of the organ grinder. Such city sounds were never a part of country life, but on Fridays, hucksters usually gathered on the village green to sell their products from wagon or truck.

In our small hamlet, as elsewhere in the Northern Neck, in truth the proverbial latchkey was always out. Whether an abundant dinner, or a simple supper of batter bread, salt roe herring and damson preserves, the hospitality was always the same, for there:

> The folks have got a charming way
> Of saying, "Come right in."
> There's smoke-cured ham, batter bread,
> Potatoes in the bin.

13

MAMMY

The land between the Rappahannock and Potomac rivers was made up of tracts of timber, ponds, winding creeks and farmlands of varied acreage. On a small farm called Sunnyside, my grandmother lived with her two grown daughters and Rose, the cook, while across the field in a modest little farmhouse lived Mr. Rock. Mr. Rock farmed the land, raised the vegetables and tended the stock. For that matter, he was called on for all manner of chores about the place. Indeed, he pretty much saw to everything, and my grandmother said, "T'would be like losing my right arm should anything happen to Mr. Rock."

My grandmother, better known as Mammy, though many years a widow, never departed from the custom of wearing mourning. Her ankle length black skirts varied in weight and texture according to the season. Her black shirtwaist, unadorned except for a white ruche at the neck, was habitually pinned by gold brooch with tracings of black enamel. It appeared her one concession to change was in summer, when a stiff brimmed black cloth hat, trimmed with a tight round flower of the same material, replaced the close fitting black bonnet and flowing veil. How well I remember her coming into the village on errands of one kind or another, and to church on Sunday morning, driving the old white horse, Dexter, harnessed to her small buggy.

From the highway, the entrance to Sunnyside was a narrow lane through open fields, windswept and cold in winter, oppressively hot in summer—more especially when shut in by tall green corn. I can still remember the smell of ripening ears with their flat green blades and tassels of yellow silk. Finally, one came into the open with clouds of dust rising beneath the horses' hooves when nearing the white frame house. Three great chestnut trees standing together just outside the yard fence were a landmark of sorts locally, for each fall my grandmother invited the village people for what she called "a chestnut hunt." The half opened burrs were strewn beneath the trees. Men with long poles flogged the top branches, showering down any left. Supplied with paper bags, each and all collected his lot. The prickly burrs and their satin brown nuts within a creamy lining now belong to the past, for the American chestnut has all but disappeared. Its smaller counterpart, the chinquapin, is still found on low bushes beside ditch banks. In addition to roasting these, as you would a chestnut, small girls strung the tiny nuts into chains to wear Indian fashion about their necks and wrists.

On entering the hall in my grandmother's house, one was usually greeted by the savory smell of fresh bread baking in the wood range, and a visit to Rose in the kitchen resulted in a buttered roll spread with preserves. One step down from the center front hall was the lower bedroom Mammy called "the chamber." It was a comfortable room, embossed white spread on the high poster bed, with folded red quilt at the foot, and a high mantle, with Seth Thomas clock of figured porcelain. Upon the white bureau scarf, edged with tatting, were those personal effects such as a pincushion with embroidered top and scalloped skirt, a silver buttonhook and shoe horn. There was a china hatpin holder and a glass container with a silver top for powder, another for loose hair. There could be a discarded jabot and, likely as not, a ripe red apple. Family snapshots were tucked in the frame of the mirror, and hanging to each side were plaster of Paris ovals, decorated with Gibson Girl cut outs, a form of decoupage popular in that time. The large flowered wash basin and pitcher sat on a marble topped washstand, and Mammy's high backed rocker, draped with a knitted afghan, was pulled near the chimney. Overall was the smell of Mentholatum and ripe fruit.

MAMMY

It was altogether different, that intimate warmth of the bedroom, the dining room and the kitchen, from the windowless cold front hall and seldom used parlor. Just inside the hall door a mounted deer's head stared with lifeless black eyes, its stiff antlers casting distorted shadows on the bare wall. One would scamper quickly past, sending it a backward look when reaching the security of Mammy's bedroom. Would it follow? What was it about the hairy neck and head, the lifeless eyes, which seemed accusing? Perhaps it had to do with its belonging in the shadowy land of departed animals and not in my grandmother's hall. And there was the picture, "The Burial of Latané," a steel engraving of some renown found in many homes in this section of Virginia. The scene depicted a grove of trees and the flag draped coffin of a confederate soldier near an open grave, the latter most likely dug by the slave nearby, leaning on a shovel. The Service was being read by the central figure, a lady of that era who, along with other sorrowing females that comprised the picture, were ancestors of prominent families of this Tidewater area. The melancholy picture, hanging above a stiff horse hair sofa in the old fashioned parlor, was made more eerie by dim bars of light that flickered through half closed blinds on the silent group.

New Year's Day our family and other relatives living nearby gathered in the pleasant dining room at Sunnyside for midday dinner. The familiar dining table, with extra leaves added and white linen cloth, held a centerpiece of evergreens and New Year's candles. At the head of the table my grandmother sat, the place designated by a heavy silver napkin ring with rolled damask napkin. It had been my grandfather's. To our delight we children were arranged at side tables on assorted chairs, with a big dictionary to lift the smallest to table height. Dinner was brought from the kitchen annex through a passageway, stuffy with the smell of old wood and drifting odors of foods. Against a wall a walnut buffet contained odds and ends of china, upon its top a well filled oil lamp. The pine cupboard, with perforated tin doors, concealed choice leftovers and sometimes a pitcher of buttermilk. The long meal wore on with its variety of dishes and heavily heaped plates. It was too long for restless children. The mingled talk of grownups about the table became a faraway, hypnotic sound conducive to sleep in the overly hot room. It was well to be excused and escape to the fresh air outside.

Usually, the Sunday school Easter Egg Hunt was held at Sunnyside, and many weeks prior, ladies in the church prepared for this annual event. It was no small task blowing the meat from dozens of eggs through a tiny aperture in one end of the shell and on through an opposite opening. The shells, dyed rainbow colors, were filled with hard candy, a bit of tissue paper pasted over the larger end. There were also store bought jellybeans, cream filled chocolate eggs and chocolate and marshmallow rabbits. Each hidden nest had a slip of paper with the name of the prospective owner. It went without saying one never divulged the whereabouts of another's nest if chancing upon it. Very young children sought their hidden nests in the belief that they had been left to them by the "Easter Rabbit." For the older children, it was still a thrill to discover the hidden treasures that held their names. A nest could be found in a clump of Jonquils along the panel fence, under the rose bush beneath the dining room window, or in a tuft of grass by the well in the kitchen yard. Perhaps it might be hidden by the root of the old Mulberry, covered by a handful of leaves, or under the steps of the front porch, or tucked in a thick bed of Narcissus . . . or . . . it could be anywhere. The egg hunt was, of course, the main event of the day, but not to be overlooked were platters of cake with different icings and freezers of

MAMMY

homemade ice cream served from the long front porch.

A VIRGINIA VILLAGE

14

THE HOUSE NEXT DOOR

When growing up in my village, I often heard my elders speak of someone as "A gentleman of the old school": a term that embodies all the niceties of a gentle upbringing, as well as an inherent courtliness of manner.

In the Northern Neck, there still existed an underlying chivalry, a deference, if you will, as shown by a gentleman to one of the opposite sex. This included such fundamental things as removing one's hat in the presence of a lady, seeing her to her vehicle or door, or offering her strength and security.

All of these things bring to mind the memory of an old friend and neighbor. He was the father of my good friend and companion who, along with her devoted parents, lived in the house next door. It was a friendly house, a house of simple, gracious living, a house where I always felt at home. I would wander across our wide lawn, on across their enclosed barn lot and pasture, to the confines of their familiar yard.

There is a nostalgic meaning for me in thinking of the house next door where I spent many good—if uneventful—hours. There was the coziness of an open fire in winter, the complacency of long summer evenings on their screened front porch. I remember sitting with the three of them, late of an evening, the shadows of approaching night creeping across the yard, the shrill chirping of summer's insects in the high grass by the pasture fence, the glow of lightning bugs in the early dusk flitting among the branches of tall trees. I recall the chatter of mundane conversation, the light hearted laughter over simple things, and the over all feeling of wellbeing. More especially I think of that gentleman, father of my friend, with his bristly moustache, hesitant speech and Old World manner. He was unfailing in reaching for his hat to walk a teenager home. He was truly "a gentleman of the old school."

15

THE LAST OF PEA-TIME

Even in the sophisticated world today, old superstitions still persist, and many think it best not to ignore them. So we would not think of having a black cat shadow our path without crossing our fingers. Who would spill the salt and fail to throw a pinch over his left shoulder, walk under a ladder, or raise an umbrella in the house? It is bad luck to get up from the wrong side of the bed, and you are compelled to say "bread and butter" if you and another pass around opposite sides of anything.

It could be a belief grown out of superstition that oysters are eaten only in months containing the letter "r." It was Uncle Peter Rich, during those months, who was of as much importance to the bounty of the kitchen as Uncle Tom and his butcher shop. Uncle Peter peddled his wares from door to door: fat, sleek oysters, newly opened and lately tonged from the nearby river. Plump and shiny in their liquor, the desired quantity was ladled from a shiny metal milk bucket with a tin dipper. There have never been since oysters of such superb quality and generous portions for ten cents a quart.

An old country expression, "It was the last of pea-time and the first of frost," no doubt alluded to that interim between fall harvest and the onset of winter. It was the time when the first hoarfrost changed the green dress of summer into flaming red and gold. Fields about the countryside were lined with tepees of shocked corn stalks, and rows of neatly stacked wood awaited the buzz of a visiting saw. It was the harvest season, the season for digging potatoes from hillocks and gathering bushels of apples from back orchards. It was a time also for retrieving wool blankets from cedar closets, wool sweaters from moth balls, for sending children off to school in knitted caps with sandwiches in brown paper bags or shiny lunch tins. Homemade book bags of blue twill, which hung across their shoulders, had large pockets in each end for holding schoolbooks.

Peculiar to some parts of the country, between fall and the new year was "hog killing time." Spirals of smoke from fires back of out-sheds rose in the clear air, and men from neighboring farms came to lend a hand in the important function. The slaughtered animals (a hideous memory) hung between poles, their stiff legs protruding grotesquely from fat, pink bodies. The next step belonged to the hired butcher. Finally, the meat moved to our big basement, where Hattie or Ella had additional help for grinding, seasoning and frying the sausage, intermittently stirring vats of boiling lard. The sausage was then sealed in glass jars.

Frosty mornings inspired early trips to the rabbit trap in the backfield, belonging exclusively to my brothers and their friends. A rabbit trap was a narrow wooden box, just wide enough to lure prey through the trap door in front to a turnip or apple in the rear. I remember once there was an opossum, once an angry stray cat . . . and once a rabbit. Overcome with compassion for the frightened little creature with bulging eyes, twitching nose and trembling heart, the boys set it free. The morning walk led past a honeypod tree, the flat brown pods filled with a pulp not unlike honey. Here beneath a gnarled persimmon tree they would stop briefly for a pre-breakfast snack. The latter reminds me of an old folk tune, to the best of my knowledge handed down solely by word of mouth. Certainly I have never seen it written. The tune was a combination chant and lullaby:

> "Watch out!" sez de 'Possum, as he shake dat 'simmon tree.
> "Don't do 'at!" sez de rabbit. "Youse shaking dem on me."
> An' dey picked wid dair claws, an' dey licked dair paws,

THE LAST OF PEA-TIME

An' dey tuk a heap home to dair Ma.

A heap, oh a heap, to dair home thu de mud.
A heap, oh a heap, thu de deep…deep…deep…
To dair Ma.

There came a time in fall when cold winds sent dry leaves scuttling across roads, and bare tree limbs, stiff and stark, framed a pale moon hanging low in the sky. The night was filled with mysterious sounds, and dark shapes lurked in the shadows. It was Halloween. Once the neighborhood held its annual costume party in a musty, vacant building known as "the old granary," now decorated with autumn leaves, stacks of corn shucks and grinning jack-o-lanterns, carved from choice pumpkins. Attic trunks were looted for grotesque and befitting costumes. That night bizarre figures glided about the dimly lit building. The figures were mysterious, yet I knew who one was, for I had heard someone say. But how unreal she looked as an old woman, wearing a false face on the back of her head under the brim of a sunbonnet worn backwards. Her real face was hidden behind a net under the black ruffles of her bonnet. Which way was she really going . . . her body walking in one direction, her head bowing in the other. Could that be Mr. Montgomery, the old man with a long white beard, a gnome-like face, humped shoulders and stout walking stick? There was something vaguely familiar about the witch with tall, peaked hat and sweeping black skirt, carrying a broomstick. Was she Miss Helen? No. Miss Helen was not so tall . . . I was sure that black cat was Esther . . . or was it? The black cat had broom-straw whiskers, black stocking pulled over her head forming cat ears, yellow rings painted around slit eyes and black tights ending in a provocative tail. It seemed unbelievable that anyone could be real in that eerie assemblage, much less someone you knew. With a shiver of relief, I joined a younger, more familiar group bobbing for apples in a zinc tub. At any rate, it was my reason for composing the following childish verse:

> The witches are whispering around tonight,
>   And spirits are walking nigh;
> An old gray owl with a solemn hoot
>   Sits in a tree nearby.
>
> White faces leer from corners black,
>   Maple leaves hanging o'er;
> A black cat's hair stands straight on its back
> The goblins dance on the floor.
>
> Frogs are singing a weird chant
>   In grass by the meadow brook;
> An ant is storing its winter food
>   Somewhere in a safe little nook.
>
> An old witch sits with an evil glance
>   At all those passing by;
> She stirs green toads in a simmering pot,
>   A pale moon hangs in the sky.

With signs of approaching winter, young people in the village waited eagerly for a first freeze for millpond skating. They impatiently looked for the first snow fall, for soft whirling snowflakes chasing each other in a madcap game of tag, clinging to hair and lashes, frosting one's shoulders and covering housetops and roads. With it came the promise for coasting down steep hills and lesser inclines. It was worth an arduous climb to the top to reach, finally, a bonfire

THE LAST OF PEA-TIME

blazing between heavy logs in a clearing in the snow. Damp knickers and woolen skirts steamed in the cold air as the group circled the cheering warmth, thawing ice encrusted mittens, melting snow from galoshes. The group's bright colored caps and gay woolen scarfs on the hilltop, fringed with green pine and bent low under a mantle of white, lent a Currier and Ives setting to the winter landscape.

In the village, adults planned ahead for the long winter months. They saw to it there was plenty of canned foods stacked on pantry shelves, plenty of meat in the cone shaped meat house, wood aplenty for feeding the maw of the kitchen range and other stoves about

VILLAGE IN WINTER

the house. One never knew what was in store for the months ahead. Somehow, back in the days of my childhood, winter sky seemed always more leaden, winter air more breathtakingly frigid, and snow decidedly deeper. Old timers remembered when the winter was "that hard" the snow was even with the fence tops and lay hard packed on roadways well into spring. With sagging, ice laden wires and felled telephone poles, all communication was cut off to the outside, evincing the severity of the winter. Snowbound, vulnerable to the throes of nature, the village then had to rely on its own resources.

Even in the dead of winter some must turn their thoughts to the needs of the summer to come, and the importance of filling icehouses. Blocks of ice were cut from frozen ponds and carried down steep ladders to the cavernous depths of dark, underground chambers, then covered with straw and sawdust. The relatively few privately owned icehouses were of benefit not only to the owners but also to others in the community, for this treasured commodity was shared, especially in times of illness.

It was in spring that a day was set aside for the sheepshearer on his annual rounds. The sheep, herded into our spacious barn, were shorn of their white coats. I recall the bags of wool shipped to Baltimore on the steamboat. There the wool was cleaned and prepared, and some of it made into soft woolen blankets with striped borders. The remainder of the prepared wool was returned from Baltimore for filling brightly colored quilts of gay, flowered chintz.

In this remote section, benighted beliefs and superstitions persisted. During the "long season in May," clusters of sweet, white bloom hung on locust trees, scenting the air with their heavy fragrance, a forerunner of the Locust Storms, the season's first thunderstorms that brought dark clouds, flashing lightning and heavy rain. Old timers called it the "breaking up of winter," after which the weather settled and summer was upon us. We children looked forward to this time, for only then were we permitted to shed winter underwear and turn out our bare feet to the field of cool grass.

It was a truly wonderful addition to the comfort and ease of our daily lives when an enterprising citizen established a plant for manufacturing ice. I recall the wooden box built for an ice chest

THE LAST OF PEA-TIME

that sat on our back porch. Large blocks of ice were delivered to us here, and we enjoyed for the first time in summer firm mounds of butter, jars of cold milk and cream, perishables of all kinds. It seems hard to realize there was ice at hand for teas and lemonade, ice for freezing the much- loved homemade ice cream.

The "Dog Days" of August brought long stretches of stifling heat, broken only by the refreshing cool of a thunderstorm. Because it was said that noise and drafts attracted lightning, we were made to sit quietly in our big front hall until the storm was over. Unfortunately for us children, during "Dog Days" we were denied a much-desired swim in the relatively cool waters of the nearby rivers. It was a widely held idea that the waters were conducive to malaria during this period. Indeed the very name "Dog Days" took on a sinister meaning for us.

A VIRGINIA VILLAGE

16
KITH AND KIN

For everybody's kith and kin in the good old Northern Neck." It could be there is more truth than poetry in the preceding, for indeed it has been said if one dipped far enough into the proverbial family tree, he might find no few of us here on this peninsula are kin—distant perhaps, but kin. The Northern Neck obviously was a great deal more isolated at the time it was settled by our ancestors some three hundred years ago, and inter marriage amongst the settlers was inevitable. In this remote country, many customs and expressions have endured through the centuries, such as the expression, "kissing cousins." The term denotes especially close kinship, and a custom of kissing as a sign of friendship and affection upon meeting and taking leave. So, it stands to reason that in a people delightfully clannish and warmly affectionate the custom is broadly practiced even today.

Once such display of "kinship" created an amusing incident in our family. On that day some cousins (elderly ladies) had come to call with their brother, who was visiting them. On leaving, my father, as was his habit, walked with them to their car and made the usual round of "good bye kissing." "It was his moustache," Papa chuckled foolishly on returning to the house. "I didn't know I kissed Phil until I felt his moustache tickle."

There were cousins who lived at Belle Ville—closely kin. They were "kissing cousins." Driving up the long lane to their invitingly attractive home, one arrived at the high front porch, with entrance on the second floor of the delightful old brick house with its English basement dining room. This is the home of a family whose roots go deep into Virginia soil. Retiring, gentle, kind, they took a faithful interest in their church, an active part in the life of the community. Dedicated, Christian people, they were benefactors of the sick and the needy.

At Belle Ville, among the many things I think of, was the greenhouse, with potted plants in all stages of growth. Perhaps because they are a favorite of mine, the geraniums stand out clearly in my picture memory: delicate pink and deep red blooms nodding behind glass panes. There are, of course, many things of far greater importance I associate with Belle Ville; as an example, the handsome silver in the pleasant basement dining room where the inviting table revealed gracious hospitality to a host of relatives and friends. Many partook of their excellent cooking and bountiful repasts. It was said that anything from the kitchen at Belle Ville was "fit for a King."

I recall the old-fashioned parlor with its high ceilings, the downstairs bedroom and the friendly cats. I remember many things pertaining to them and their home, but I especially remember the three white-haired cousins and "Liza," the youngest member of the household, whose splendid character and capable ways endeared her to family and friends.

Thanksgiving dinner at the parish house, an annual event, would not have been complete without Belle Ville's rich plum pudding and pans of spiced apples. This special dinner had a widespread reputation for its excellence, and people came from near and far on that day to partake of the fine repast put on by the ladies of the small country church. The following is a typical menu: turkey, baked or fried oysters, country ham, green peas, candied sweet potatoes, slaw, spiced apples, relishes, hot rolls, coffee, Belle Ville plum pudding with wine sauce, and ice cream—all for $1.00. Truly, the dollar then was worth its weight in gold. It was a convivial, pleasant occasion. It was a day for family gatherings. Young people, home from schools for the holiday,

KITH AND KIN

joined with their families in the crowded basement dining room of the Parish House, the hum of conversation rising above the rattle of dishes in the nearby kitchen. At this time, young girls of the church lent their youth and energy to waiting on tables. Visiting hunters and local Nimrods came from the fields and marshes, their sportsman attire adding a touch of the out-of-doors to the friendly gathering in the warm room.

Looking far back, I can remember a jousting tournament which was held at Belle Ville, an event no doubt to raise money for some special cause. Each of the riders, dubbed a knight, wore his chosen colors in a sash about his waist, streamers of the same colors fastened to the handle of his lance and laced in the bridle of his mount. There might have been a dozen entries with such colorful names as The Knight of Essex, The Knight of Westmoreland, The Knight of Stratford, The Knight of Level Green, or some other place or locality. "Knight of Cedar Grove," the Master of the tournament would call out, "Ride, Sir Knight!" With such a charge, each rider in turn thundered down the dusty lane intent on collecting three brass rings on the tip of his lance. These rings, hanging from arms of three consecutive posts bordering the lane, were twice replaced by smaller rings, thus increasing the skill required for piercing the tiny openings.

A gasp ran through the crowd of spectators as a fiery black horse, flecked with foam and glistening with sweat, sent the rider over its head. There was an interlude of uneasy waiting and quiet speculation as the local doctor elbowed his way through the huddled crowd. Finally the word, "It isn't serious," passed through the assemblage with many audible expressions of relief from the now relaxed people. The brave knight, a bit more dashing, a bit more glamorous with white bandage about his head, continued his ride under the admiring eyes of the spectators.

Booths were set up on the spacious front lawn, decorated with bunting, Queen Anne's Lace, and field daisies. It was here one could buy a glass of lemonade, dipped from a zinc tub containing a block of ice from Belle Ville's own icehouse. There were also cones of the ever-popular ice cream, scooped from home freezers. That night the lawn was lighted with Japanese lanterns and bottles with wicks in kerosene, strung from tree to tree. Rows of benches made from boards placed across overturned tomato crates faced the high front porch, transformed into a stage. A prolonged "Ahhh" arose from the audience, followed by a gasp of admiration. Folding

screens, serving as a curtain, were removed, revealing a semi-circle of Tidewater's loveliest girls. Behind each stood her gallant knight. Following some light oratory, each rider presented his lady with a

KITH AND KIN

bouquet of garden flowers. The applause accelerated into a thundering climax when the winning knight placed a floral wreath on the shinning hair of his "Queen of Love and Beauty."

A VIRGINIA VILLAGE

17
INTERIM DAYS

A brief period between boarding school and the little frame schoolhouse behind the hedge was spent in public school. This two story building, of box like construction, in retrospect seems even more inadequate and unattractive than it did then. Lack of plumbing was not confined to the one room school, for I recall two "chick sale" out houses in latticed enclosures to each side of the field behind the school building.

The field, with its dusty baseball diamond and sandbag home plate, was a popular gathering place in season for enthusiastic ball fans. Baseball was an important activity and diversion to peoples in rural areas. Everyone turned out to see the adult home team— made up of selected baseball players around the county—take on a visiting rival. The entire family, in Model T Ford or a car of like vintage, came early to be assured of the parking space in the circle surrounding home plate. There were few, if any, bleachers then, and the automobile afforded seats for the family. Men draped themselves over the cars' hoods or sat atop fenders. Children with dripping ice cream cones were contentedly perched on the wide running boards. There was heated rooting, heckling, horn blowing and other displays of enthusiastic loyalty when a member of our team made a home run or "put 'em out" on first.

Two to a desk in the crowded school room, there was hardly space to open the big "Fry's Geography," let alone see the chalk smeared blackboard behind bobbing heads and wiggling bodies. I remember the smell of chalk dust, wet leather shoes and damp woolen coats hanging on pegs along the wall, an overflow of wraps from the small cloakroom on the first floor. There was no cafeteria then, and lunchtime found desktops littered with pasteboard boxes, tin pails, paper bags and an occasional lunch box. It was a welcome, if noisy, hour.

This was a carefree age of high school romance and class work, interspersed with holidays and other activities. In spring, there was lethargy in the soft air drifting through open windows, dispelling the closeness of winter, and bringing in high-pitched voices from the playground below. It was then thoughts turned to the long awaited commencement, with its conclusion of months of work now past, its promise of unknown things to come. There was tense excitement mixed with a feeling of nostalgia for those leaving forever the familiar old school.

The one commencement I seem to remember was when my older sister, though too young to be among the graduates, was given a part in the closing exercises. In white eyelet dress, a white ribbon in her dark hair, she recited Longfellow's "The Building of the Ship." It began, "Like unto ships far off at sea, // Outward or homeward bound, are we." It was the following lines I especially liked and remember: "Before, behind, and all around, // Floats and swings the horizon's bound." It was here my sister, with a sweep of her arms, dramatically portrayed the limitless sea.

World War I was upon us, and patriotism was at fever pitch throughout the land. The dreadful war had drawn the world closer together, and our boys in trim khaki uniforms were leaving for the theater of operations overseas. The local post office, indeed most public buildings, displayed war posters . . . lovely girls in white uniforms with bright red crosses on their flowing headdress. There was Uncle Sam in high silk hat with a band of stars, pointing his index finger from a star-spangled cuff. The caption called for volunteers. Like other small children, perhaps, I knew a feeling of affection for this Uncle Sam, this glorified uncle of sorts, who held

INTERIM DAYS

us all in his safe keeping. There were many other things to indicate our country was at war, such as the list posted on the courthouse door with the names of all those young men from the county who were drawn into the conflict. This list was scanned feverishly by relative and friend who had, or knew, someone "over there." The silver star by a name denoted "Wounded in Battle," a gold star, "The Supreme Sacrifice." These brave young men were always upper-most in the hearts and minds of those at home, regardless of race or creed. The Red Cross room, set up in a vacant office above the bank, seethed with volunteer workers. Even children, anxious to do their part, knitted wristlets, rolled bandages, and made candles from tightly rolled newspapers dipped in tallow.

Once some children in the village conceived their own entertainment to make money for the Red Cross, each displaying his or her specialty in song or skit. I remember my brother, with his freckle-faced companion, dressed in Scout uniforms, singing:

> I want to be a soldier boy
> And in the army fight,
> For this my own dear native land,
> With all my strength and might.

It was Lucy who sang the sentimental ditty:

> My papa's all dressed up today,
> Dressed up oh so fine.
> I thought when I first looked at him,
> My papa wasn't mine.

It concluded with the following lines:

> But his buttons are marked U.S.,
> And that spells us, I guess,
> So he still belongs to dear Ma-Ma and me.

A VIRGINIA VILLAGE

Any excuse brought out a parade with floats, flags, bunting, and a brass band recruited from the nearest military camp. Here shiny instruments, colorful uniforms and rolling drums contributed to the patriotic theme of the day, where many people of the community took part in the locally conceived floats. Draped in a white sheet on a flag-bedecked truck, a crown of gilded pasteboard upon her long black hair, the Statue of Liberty, arms extended upward, clutched in her hand a torch of shiny tinfoil. Nearby, wearing a frock coat and tall hat banded with stars, his long legs encased in striped red, white and blue pants, was our Uncle Sam.

There was other entertainment besides the parade and band music, such as singing by a local quartet, with special emphasis on patriotic songs: "'Til We Meet Again," "Johnny Get Your Gun," "Keep the Home Fires Burning." It was when the quartet bore down on the sentimental "Just Break the News to Mother," there was hardly a dry eye. One of our leading citizens, or some politician adept at oratory, made the important address of the day. From a stand draped in red, white and blue bunting, his voice rang out with patriotic zeal over the rapt audience. Never since has such fervor, such depth of feeling, such love of country, been so universally manifest as in those days.

My brother had a part in the long day's events, for he, too, made an impassioned speech. A lad of some twelve years, in a borrowed uniform, his legs wrapped in olive-colored puttees above snub-toed shoes, his scrubbed face shinning with concentrated effort, he delivered the following brief speech, written for him by the principal of the school. It was a takeoff on Patrick Henry's famous oration:

> Ladies and Gentlemen, since we have plunged into a World War against an enemy drunk with the lust for power, I ask, shall we meekly

INTERIM DAYS

submit, shall we resort to entreaty or humble supplication? If so, what terms shall we find which have not already been exhausted?

The first gale that sweeps from the east brings to our ears the resounding clash of arms. Our brethren are already in the field. Why stand we here idle? Is life so dear or peace so sweet as to be purchased at the cost of chains or slavery? Forbid it, Almighty God.

I know not what course others may take, but as for me, I would rather lie in a patriot's grave than live a coward, fettered to the throne of that despotic monarch, the Kaiser.

A VIRGINIA VILLAGE

18

NORTHERN NECK NEWS

From the little frame building, the Northern Neck News, our weekly paper, enjoyed a wide circulation in and about the countryside. For that matter, it followed those who moved elsewhere as well as those of us temporarily away from home. I remember, when off at school, I looked forward each week to its arrival in the mail. Soon my friends were also enjoying the original format of my home paper.

For the most part, this paper was composed of news in and about the peninsula, and did not delve into world happenings and events. It was this that made it uniquely akin to its readers, for its pages contained news of people and places that related to, or were familiar to, most of us. They said, "It was just like a letter from home."

Aside from this very personal feature, the Northern Neck News was a source of valuable information, a barometer of what, if any changes occurred affecting this remote land and its people. It was also a register of statistics: births, marriages, and deaths. Most assuredly, the archives of this special paper are rich in the history of this peninsula.

In addition to the column of social happenings in our village, interspersed with topics such as the weather and mundane bits of news, the paper carried what were known as "weekly letters," written by different correspondents, under such

A VIRGINIA VILLAGE

colorful pseudonyms as Bob White, Jack Frost, Seldom, and Soldier. A meaningful letter from a writer in a small crossroads exemplifies these things of importance in that neighborhood:

Lyells Corner

> Fodder, hay and shucks are greatly in demand here. William Rich, colored, had the misfortune to lose a fine young ox a few days ago. Mr. Smith Webb Rock completed him a new icehouse and nearly filled it.
>
> Mrs. R. J. Hall has sold from the 20th of January to the 24th of February $8.30 worth of eggs from 47 head of hens.
>
> —*Northern Neck News* – February 28, 1908
> Reprinted February 27, 1964, Sec. 2, pg. 5.

This four page newspaper carried not only local business advertisements, but Wanted and For Sale columns, faithfully scanned by its readers. It was their market place of bargains. The following delightful advertisement in a 1918 edition of the Northern Neck News was inserted by no other than the editor himself:

FOR SALE

> I will trade or sell my mare, "Phyllis." A splendid traveler and will work well anywhere. As a traveler she has few equals. Not afraid of machines. Only one fault, will kick at times, but with careful handling this is easily avoided....
>
> —*Northern Neck News, August 2, 1918*
> Reprint 10/5/72, pg. 14, "Twice Told Tales"

The following reprint from a column in the Northern Neck News called "Twice Told Tales" sets the tone for the pace of living in the year 1918:

> Two flying machines attracted much attention here last Wednesday by landing in the river at Fleeton. Indeed, almost in the yards of those living on the waterfront. One in the morning, bound for Washington, stopped for water. About 8 o'clock in the evening another gracefully pitched in the same place. A number from Reedville and vicinity quickly made for the spot in cars and motor boats. It was well worth seeing the beautiful planes rise up from the water's edge and sweep off until lost in cloudy space Southward.
>
> —*Northern Neck News, 08/2/1918*
> Reprint 10/5/1972, pg. 14

Held with both fondness and respect, he was, without a doubt, one of our best known citizens, the owner and editor of our local paper. In spite of the problems of transportation as once existed, he was usually at all important gatherings, mingling with the people he knew so well, gleaning news for his paper, extending its circulation. A debonair, courtly gentleman, he was known and loved by a host of friends and acquaintances. The gay flower in the buttonhole of his lapel, a habitual part of his attire, was as much associated with him as his usual courtesy and friendly handshake: a southern gentleman. His paper, the Northern Neck News, reached far into the past to days of the horse and buggy, the awakening of the machine age and the first automobile, to today's world of the atomic bomb.

Ably carried on by his grandson, the Northern Neck News has grown greatly in size and circulation. Even today, it reflects little the frenzied rushing tide of world happenings. Expanded enough to keep abreast of a growing local population, it maintains almost the same format. It is still, "Just like a letter from home."

A VIRGINIA VILLAGE

19

GROWING PAINS

Teen days: carefree days of growing up. Days of fun and laughter, of heartthrobs and heart aches . . . days of youth, when nothing seemed more important than the pursuit of pleasure.

Inevitably came those hot days of summer that enveloped the village in a languor and inertia. The elderly sought the dubious cool of a darkened room behind drawn shades, but the restless young continued to seek companionship and entertainment. Young girls in freshly starched muslin, a matching ribbon about their hair, wandered in pairs down the narrow dirt sidewalk to the village drug store. This, having replaced Mr. Garland's ice cream parlor, was now the popular gathering place. It was a pleasant drug store, with round, marble topped tables, wire backed chairs, and a big wooden fan slowly revolving in the high ceiling. Of most importance, it had the first soda fountain for miles about, with counter of polished marble and gleaming spigots. Here one might obtain a delectable new drink called Coca Cola, a malted milk, banana split or tin roof—the latter comprising a dip of ice cream, with chocolate syrup, marshmallow whip and nuts. It was a foregone conclusion that most of the young would come there some time during the afternoon. Boys joined girls about the tables to talk over the last dance, make a date for the one forthcoming, and discuss the latest popular record. With a scuffling of feet and scraping of chairs, younger lads sought a corner table, exchanged jabs in one another's ribs, and blew jackets from soda straws to attract attention. Some had a small cluster of wild flowers on their caps where the top snapped to the visor. I recall a small knot of pink arbutus, a wild violet or two, a bloom of red clover, and once a single head of wheat extending stiffly across the brim. I am not sure whether this fad had any significance. I am sure it related only to those in the country.

With the coming of fall, most of these young people diverted to boarding schools and colleges. The roads un-surfaced, sometimes impassable for the drafty, top-heavy bus, the steamboat remained a reliable source of travel. Many would leave at the same time from the nearest boat landing for Fredericksburg, and from there, head in different directions for their respective schools.

Most familiar in the Northern Neck were the steamers: "Lancaster," "Middlesex," "Potomac," and "Three Rivers," which plied the Rappahannock and Potomac, then up the Bay to Baltimore. Sounding a stentorian signal, they called at each wharf, and from their cavernous interior, stevedores trundled one-wheeled carts of freight.

Aside from the deck, the gathering place on the steamboat for social activities was the saloon, its worn red carpet smelling of stale tobacco. Two brass posts, connected by heavy red cord with gold tassels, marked the flight of stairs to the above deck. Tubs of rubber plants stood at each corner.

Second only in importance to the captain was the purser, who dealt with such things as invoices, tickets and other matters pertaining to money. I can still remember one, a dour man with leathery skin and a gold front tooth, seated behind the iron bars of his small cage. Finally there was the captain, with tarnished gold braid on his worn blue serge, a brimmed cap with gold insignia, and a heavy watch chain across his wide girth. Overall he had an air of dependability and importance.

There is an unforgettable memory of those old riverboats with their bare necessities and respectable decor. They have an important place in the nostalgic past. There was, of course, the dining room and its tables covered with white cotton cloths. Just inside the door, a small stand held a bulging water cooler with one turned-over drinking glass near by. I recall the staterooms with their lingering smell of shaving soap, dank cotton blankets, and a faint odor of carbolic acid.

Winter followed close on the heels of fall, and Christmas on the heels of winter. That holiday season found the small drug store crowded again with those home on vacation. Wools and tweeds replaced linens and muslin, and one noticed a sprig of mistletoe or holly instead of arbutus or violets. This was the day when the popular band of Guy Lombardo played "The Sweetest Music This Side of Heaven" for the college prom. There were other fine orchestras, such as Wayne King and K. Kaiser, which also had their place in the limelight.

Winter holidays and summer vacations were highlighted by private dances, or public-subscription dances. The latter varied in

A VIRGINIA VILLAGE

accordance with the cost of the band hired from some nearby city. Tickets were sold at the door. At times parents of the dance committee contributed trays of homemade sandwiches to be sold at intermission, helping defray costs as well as satisfy hunger.

Prior to such an occasion, our house buzzed with activity. White linen suits, freshly laundered, were fetched from Aunt Bell Turner, who was especially good at "doing them up." Aunt Bell, just out from the village a ways, also attempted dry cleaning of a sort, albeit the odor of gasoline lingered for some time. Closet doors in the big bedrooms were hung with billowing organdie and crisp dotted Swiss, while colored slippers nearby awaited a Cinderella foot.

Teen days: carefree days of growing up. With so much of the past stored in my mind, it is hard to understand why a time of no special importance should rise to the surface. There was really nothing to set it apart, that evening preceding a dance. It was that time already when the day stood on the "edge of dark," and young men, our dates for the evening, were beginning to arrive. The ends of their cigarettes glowed in the descending darkness on our side porch as I joined them. Inexplicably, the side porch seemed to come into a different focus, and I saw it through different eyes. In retrospect, there was a new awareness of the familiar wicker furniture, an unprecedented tenderness for the old Safrano rose, shedding its petals by the porch steps. There was magic in the summer moonlight, transforming everyday landscapes and homely surroundings into mellow gray and gold. A movement of breeze in the leaves of the old locust caressed my cheek, disturbed my bobbed hair, played briefly with the ruffles on the hem of my long party dress. As you can see, there was really nothing special to set the night apart excepting, perhaps, the night itself: a stirring of naïve fantasies of youth, the expectant dreams of an unknown future. All to do with being young.

Our high school auditorium, floor waxed to a super gloss, was decorated with streamers of crepe paper and clusters of low-hanging balloons. As I remember, there was no greater thrill than that first step onto the dance floor, a wailing saxophone in your ears and the expectant stag line against the wall. The popular "break dance" was in vogue, and a girl needed to be most adept at changing steps from a tall partner to one of lesser height, the latter facilitating the intimate "cheek dance." From a loping arm-pumper to the smooth, rhythmic steps of another, one swayed, hopped, glided about the floor. "Yes, We Have No Bananas" laughed the trombone; "Wang, Wang Blues" mourned the saxophone; "Girl of My Dreams" crooned the mellow clarinet. So the happy evening advanced to a late hour and the inevitable strains of "Home, Sweet Home." In response to whistles and hand clapping, the band gave a series of encores, ending this time with "Goodnight, Sweetheart" or "Auf Wiedersehen." As a final resort, a hat was passed: an inducement, a bait for the tired musicians who obliged once again. The time came, however, when one knew the night must "let go." Early morning fatigue enveloped the dancers and the now faltering notes of the instruments. Even the big drum bespoke a weariness. Young men found their dates for the final dance, which ended a perfect evening.

A VIRGINIA VILLAGE

20

STORY BOOK HOUSE

Tied in historically with the early life and families of this Tidewater peninsula, Bladensfield, though perhaps not so well known as some other places, is equally as interesting. For that matter, it is older. Certainly it is one of the oldest houses in this area, having been built around 1690 for one John Jenkins, who

in 1655 was granted a thousand acres of land by Governor Barnett for bringing twenty settlers to Virginia.

On entering the long driveway or lane, bordered by a stand of bamboo, overhanging cedars and other indigenous growth, one approaches the interesting old house in its setting of ancient trees and shrubs. Scattered about the spacious front yard is the rough grained fruit from the pomegranate tree, and to the back of the house, a profusion of bloom adds a spot of color to the old fashioned garden,

A VIRGINIA VILLAGE

preserved for over two centuries. The long, gray frame house is of an unusual construction known as noggin; that is, its brick walls are covered with weatherboarding. With its steep roof, tall chimneys and many dormers, Bladensfield has a distinction all its own.

Double doors at each end of the hall have bars of hand-hewn timber which serve as locks, and in at least one door frame is an ancient Indian peephole. A treasured lamp hangs in that hall, dating back two hundred years or more. One finds in the adjoining rooms lovely hand-carved mantles and the well-known H & L hinges, believed to keep out evil spirits. It is fascinating to learn that a silver ladle belonging to the family was buried during the Revolutionary War in the vegetable garden beneath the cabbage patch.

There was a time when the owners of Bladensfield were three aristocratic, silver-haired old ladies who, with their sweeping black skirts, frilly shirtwaists and high lace collars, looked as though they had stepped out of the eighteenth century. I remember when Bladensfield sheltered three generations under its steep roof. An interesting household, consisting of the elderly aunts, their nephew (a courtly and learned gentleman), and his widowed sister with her four handsome children. I recall especially one little girl, with wide gray eyes, a tangle of light gold hair, and exquisite coloring. Barefoot, in faded cotton dress, she stood framed in the hall doorway, holding in her arms a white rabbit. With the innocence of youth lending an added purity to her natural beauty, she was a subject for any artist's brush. Fate deemed she would become a famous New York model, a far contrast to that child in a rural setting long ago.

Once some of us in the village were invited by the friendly young man from Bladensfield on a hay ride of sorts in his big farm

STORY BOOK HOUSE

truck, "Samson." It was, of course, inevitable that it would end at that charming old place—thus creating another memorable evening. Darkness was falling as we approached the house, with the faint outline of a full moon rising over its steep gables, and gnarled old trees sending fingers of shadow across the dimming lawn. Bathed in soft moonlight, the old house sat resigned and serene, like an aged, gray lady filled with enduring memories.

Inside, a bright fire, cheering and inviting, blazed on the open hearth that chilly evening in early fall. We pulled close to the warmth of the lapping flames to avoid drafts seeping across door sills, and the better to roast marshmallows on forked sticks over glowing coals, and shake the corn, popping in a wire basket with long handle. In such a setting, what could have been a more delightful climax than to have one of the aunts, dear little Miss Evie, charm us with stories of the past—remembrances of her early days during the Civil War. Indeed, it is my memory that is hazy, for I can only recall one tale she recounted that evening. It was during the Sixties, and a servant girl answering a knock on the hall door saw a group of Yankee soldiers outside. The frightened girl let fall the heavy cross bar and rushed upstairs screaming to her mistress. The floor bears to this day the scar where it fell.

In measured time the years reached ahead, leaving in their wake remembrances of happenings and events: sharp picture memories stored in the corners of the mind. Such was one special morning in early spring. The double doors on each side of the hall opened and closed repeatedly: closed to the lingering cold of winter; opened to welcome those who came from near and afar. They came with final respect for the master of Bladensfield. The years had dealt kindly with him, for he died at a ripe old age here in this place he loved so well. A feeling of tranquility seemed to envelop the old house, extending beyond to the untilled, sleeping

A VIRGINIA VILLAGE

fields. Already the swelling buds on the fringe of trees along the edge of the woods displayed their first tender, green leaves. Here and there in the dormant flower borders a brave crocus showed its yellow head. Relatives and friends, old and young, colored and white, formed a procession behind the minister from the adjacent village church. A fickle wind roughed his hair and made billowing clouds of his white surplice as he led us across the field to an adjacent wood. There in a clearing beside a still pond, the wooden casket came to rest. Upon its top stretched a simple branch of pine, its waxy green needles redolent with the sap of life. The silence was broken only by the whispering of the wind in the tall pines above; then, the voice of the minister repeating the familiar and comforting words of the burial service. "The pine branch was nice," I said to one of his daughters who was walking beside me back to the empty house. "Your father would have liked it." "Yes," she replied simply, "only this morning I got it from the woods."

Although the old house hasn't changed much in appearance, there have been changes of occupancy, though it still remains in the same family. Today, one might uncover many true stories and legends woven about this ancient place and the generations that lived there.

This is a country rich in delightful lore, such as the episode Miss Evie recounted from the Civil War that evening in Bladensfield. I recall another true story relating to the Civil War told to me by my great aunt, that took place not in Bladensfield, but in my ancestral home of Edgehill. She was a little girl, a frightened little girl who had hidden in the clothes hamper that day when the Northern soldiers came to Edgehill. Many of the valuables and family heirlooms were already buried for safe keeping in the vegetable garden. Even the small mahogany chest with tortoise shell drawers and silver handles and pulls was safely buried with the flat silver. It was said that this same chest was buried twice before in a like manner. Ransacking the stately old brick house, the soldiers came upon the clothes hamper in a linen closet. A young officer hoisted the frightened and tearful little girl to his shoulder. Her tears stopped when he offered her a piece of peppermint candy, the likes of which were rarely seen then in any Southern home. They started afresh when her proud and wary mama forbade her have it.

A VIRGINIA VILLAGE

21
ORGAN MUSIC

Sarah and Walter came to live in the little house on the edge of the clover field. They stayed the rest of their lives, raised a family of seven, and became an integral part of the daily life of our place. Walter worked the small farm back of our big house and took care of the stock and vegetable garden. More especially, he became a respected citizen in the community.

For no real reason, the head of our back stairs was his chosen place for any important communication with our family. It was there he came to ask Mama if 'twas anything she wanted done "special" about the house or yard. "I is pretty much caught up out back and has a little time." One day he came to announce the arrival of his last little boy, adding proudly, "He gonna be named Joe after the Jedge." It was here Walter came on Christmas morning to collect his presents and have his important Christmas drink with Papa. "Merry Christmas, Walter," Papa would say, pouring a sizable drink of bourbon in a water glass—a small jigger for himself. "And I wish you and your family good health and happiness for the coming year." "Yes sir, Jedge," Walter replied, tilting the glass to his mouth. "And the same to you," he said, smacking his lips and grinning. "Now the day's got started right!"

As much or more than anywhere else, the back stairs played an important part in our everyday life. It was up these stairs Walter carried armfuls of wood to the high back box in the upper hall, wood for the King heaters in the six bedrooms. I recall the crackles of a newly lit fire in the early morning, the tip of my cold nose protruding from a mound of warm blankets; and later scampering through chilly halls for breakfast in the bright, warm dining room. It was these same stairs we children raced down, out through the door at the foot, to the cool of summer in the side yard.

Nothing pleased Sarah and Walter so much as a visit from one of our family, and we were proudly ushered into their small parlor with the snuff brown sofa from our back sitting room, and a rug patterned with sprawling pink roses. Although there was no chimney outlet, a tall ornate stove stood mid center of the room. Beside the window, hung with Mama's lace curtains, an overstuffed chair was protected by a plastic cover. But it was in the warm, uncluttered kitchen I liked to visit, a chair pulled up to a table covered with white oilcloth. In a glass bottle, an artificial flower lent a spot of color. Hanging over the room was the good smell of apples bubbling on the kitchen stove, stirred by Sarah with a wooden spoon.

It was, however, the organ that was their prized possession, the old organ from our back hall. Walter had "spoken for it" if it was ever decided to "let her go." He came for it one summer evening in the spring wagon, along with little Joe, the latter's face alive with happiness, his voice quivering with suppressed excitement. They left with it by way of the lane, out to the highway and on to the side road leading to his house. Oblivious to what impression he made on those he passed, Walter succumbed to the delight of ownership. Seated on a chair before the organ, undisturbed by the creaking wagon, he joyously played and sang his way home. It would be hard to say who was the happier, the old man or the small boy, his face shining beneath the brim of his straw hat—for "little Joe" was given for the first time responsibility of driving the aged horse. Later, the parlor wall behind the organ was hung with pictures of their family, including Sarah and Walter, stiffly posed on their wedding day. The

ORGAN MUSIC

organ top was reserved for photographs of "Miss Sally" (my mother) and "The Jedge," along with a few other pictures of the family, some given, some retrieved from trash cans.

A real rapport existed between our family and theirs. After Mama died, I remember Sarah saying, "Not meaning any harm, I think I is the closest to a grandmother you all has got, if you know what I mean." I did know. Having lost our mother and also those special aunts so much a part of our household, she was now the oldest woman left on the place.

Walter was a Deacon in his church, a position of no little importance; but in later years he was content to make his peace with God in the great out-of-doors. Often he was overheard speaking out loud to the Lord as he went about his chores. Once a young lad in our village, bent on a youthful search for pigeons in the loft of our big barn, chanced to hear from below the old man's voice as it rose through the cracks in the floor. It was lifted in humble prayer to his Maker. With great sensitivity, not wishing to disturb so private a moment, the boy remained motionless and silent. Years later this episode, beautifully written, appeared in our local newspaper.

It is unfortunate no one wrote down Walter's homespun philosophies, rich in color and meaningful truths. Many of his thoughts had to do with Man and Nature, intertwined in some inimitable way, now for the most part too fragmented to recall in whole. In his late years when his health was declining, he put it this way: "I can't say I is as pert as I has been, but there's a lot of music left in this old box yet."

Eventually confined to his bedroom in the little house in the corner of the clover field, he had little use that Christmas for anything related to his once normal activities, and his simple needs were well cared for. We wondered what gift would brighten his Christmas. Always thoughtful, it was my younger sister who suggested the "money tree," and living nearby, she volunteered to deliver it. It was late Christmas Eve, and the snow that blanketed the surrounding country had ceased falling, leaving fields around the little house an expanse of frozen white. Under the crisp, bright stars, my sister and her young daughter braved the frigid night, holding high the small "money tree." From the kitchen window of the little frame house, an oil lamp sent a band of yellow light through the darkness, marking a pathway to the door. On the branches of the small tree, firmly planted in a wooden bucket, hung shining balls of silver and red. The gay Christmas cards were secured to the branches with red ribbons, each tiny envelope holding a "money gift" from members of his family, as he called us.

It was his last Christmas. Early the following year, neighbors both white and colored, paid him their respects in the small church of his past. The "old music box" had played out. An old friend was gone.

22

MISS SALLY

Devoting no few years to five babies in stair step ages of one through seven, she gained too much weight. Though this somewhat hampered her activity, it in no way affected her joyous disposition. Free of affectation, she had little interest in superficial things, such as the latest in fashion or dress. The white hair, framing her soft brown eyes and animated face, was likely as not in casual disarray. Known generally as Miss Sally, her pleasure was in simple things, her interest in all people. With her, there was no generation gap, and her warm personality reached out to all ages, to all walks of life, receiving in return love, respect, and admiration. Surely she was one of the few who, to quote Kipling, could " . . . walk with kings nor lose the common touch." Overall, she maintained a certain reserve, sensed rather than deliberately shown, especially concerning her family and loved ones. Although wanted and invited, her acceptance of invitations was rare, and it was a tribute of their love and esteem that friends sought her in her own home.

An early riser, she awaited each of us for breakfast in the sunny dining room, coffee cups spread before her, the fat silver sugar bowl and cream pitcher at her right. The evening meal was the time our large family was most likely to all be together. Then lively discussions and exchanges of ideas were in order, lasting long after the table had been cleared. Midday, more likely than not there was someone aside from the family whose plate had been hastily added. Perhaps cousins, who had dropped by when in the village and stayed for dinner or lunch, perhaps a lawyer or business acquaintance of Papa's, perhaps some other relative or friend. Always included as family would be an unmarried or widowed aunt, either or both making a

A VIRGINIA VILLAGE

part-time home with us. This may show to some extent the unity—but confusion—of life in our big house, over which extended my mother's enveloping love and hospitality.

There were times when there were specially invited guests for dinner, when the long mahogany table was set with the best linen and china, and we children had an early meal about the old walnut table in the kitchen. I can remember one time, when I was seven years old, I diligently sewed through the day, lovingly making a red rose from a bit of calico: a surprise for my mother to wear that night. "But what will you do? You surely cannot wear it," I heard my little aunt say. Later, however, peeping through the spokes of the stair railing in the upstairs hall, this small girl's eyes shown with love and admiration. Securely pinned in her mother's hair was the red rose. It could have been a diamond tiara she wore along with her braided black silk dress, she looked that regal. She was unconcerned as she descended the stairs to greet her guests, her merry laugh floating upward.

Cajoled and prodded by insistent children, she once attended with Papa a large, formal banquet in nearby Richmond. She vowed it was the kind of thing she "did not really care for," a statement meant in all sincerity but, as had often happened, once she arrived at the place, she enjoyed it and was enjoyed by all. It was easy to spot her from the balcony that overlooked the brilliantly lit room. Animated and handsome in her black lace with shawl, her natural charm drew old friends who brought others to meet Miss Sally.

In her late life, it was an afternoon drive with some of her family that became her chosen diversion and, because of their mutual love for music, songs poured from open windows of the old sedan as they drove about the countryside. Some were current songs, but mostly they were the old songs of her day: "I'll Deck My Hair With Roses," "Beautiful Dreamer," and "After the Ball."

MISS SALLY

There was the quaint old favorite, "The Man in the Moon," with words something like this:

> The man in the moon is winking
> As he sits in his old armchair;
> And what is that old man thinking,
> I wish he'd stop winking at me.
>
> Chorus
> Love, I will love you ever,
> Love, I will leave you never,
> Ever to be, faithful to thee,
> Never to say goodbye.

Except for occasional attendance at her church, where her rich contralto filled the bare spots in the struggling little choir, she preferred the shade of the old locust tree in the side yard, the cool of the big front hall—the bosom of her family. How true what was said of her: "Her home is her castle; her mantle, love."

It was she who was the pivot about which the family revolved, who established meaningful traditions and rich, colorful memories. Hers is a spirit that remains eternal, in the flowering of the trees in spring, the fall of winter snow . . . at Easter, at Christmas . . . throughout the seasons. Her presence touches yesterday, today and tomorrow.

A VIRGINIA VILLAGE

23

CHRISTMAS

There is no recollection of my childhood more filled with nostalgia than the Christmas season, as I remember it with my parents and my brothers and sisters in our big country house. It is this season, this very special holiday season, that brings floods of memories as I recall the sounds, the smells, the underlying excitement that prevailed.

It was the time for many visits to the country stores, their windows dressed in holiday attire. Sparkling loops of tinsel and streamers of red crepe paper draped the dingy glass windowpanes, along with the patches of simulated snow. Mid center in the steaming window might well be a shiny sled with red runners, a sprig of holly painted on the top. Along with other toys, it took precedence over such mundane things as a zinc tub, stacked boxes of gun shells, a keg of nails, now relegated to the back of the window.

Inside was a wonderland of gifts from which to choose, placed on counter tops within easy sight of young eyes: sling shots, paint sets, story books, toy soldiers, dolls with painted faces and cloth bodies stuffed with sawdust. There could be a cardboard house, gleaming ice skates, a china tea set, and perhaps a tiny iron cook stove like the real one in our kitchen. Out of all of this, I seem to remember it was a character doll from the local store that was the dearest to my heart, more even than the lovely French doll my father had ordered from the city, with bisque body and real hair.

It was a time for noting each exciting package that disappeared somewhere within the depths of the big house under mama's watchful care. There was added exhilaration upon catching a glimpse of red ribbon through the half closed door of the Christmas room and hearing the crinkle of paper wrappings. Did one also hear the tinkle of a toy piano, the clang of a windup train? Most anything could happen this enchanted season, when small ears were attuned to the sounds of Christmas, when eyes held stars of wonder, and an unfaltering belief lived in the hearts of children. For the young, it was a time of happy suspense as they dreamed of a jolly old elf in a red suit, and it was a time also for being on one's best behavior.

It was a time for evergreens, snowflakes and holly berries, for bringing in the tall cedar to the front hall to be strung with baubles and tinsel, of fetching down armfuls of gaily tied packages to place beneath its bedecked boughs. There were garlands of running cedar to be carried to the four corners of the hall, with a cherished sprig of mistletoe to hang from the center light. There were wreaths for doors, and bunches of holly and pine placed behind pictures, with containers of graceful swamp berries to add to the gala decorations.

Last, but not least, hanging like a promise in the air, were the smells of Christmas. The freshness of evergreens mingled with the odors from the kitchen. The pungent smell of spices in round cookies, the aroma of wine jelly and fruitcake, brandied sweet potato pudding and eggnog, blended with the smell of the big turkey roasting in the wood range. It was at this special time that my mother saw to it that each and every one had his or her favorite sweet from the kitchen. There was a golden cake with jelly filling, mounds of fresh coconut on towering layers, the delectable Dolly Varden cake and, of course, the usual big fruit cake. It was after the last baking was done and the last sprig of holly was in place, when the faint winter's sun was slipping behind the frigid rim of the horizon and day was waning that the exuberance of childhood reached its pinnacle with the nearness of Christmas. Noses pressed

CHRISTMAS

against the windowpane, we watched the falling snow fill pathways and cover housetops, nature's gift to the holiday season.

Finally, bundled in bed, we listened with suppressed excitement to the opening of wooden crates on the back porch: crates of delicacies ordered from Baltimore and deposited at the nearest steamboat wharf. There were fruits and conserves, fat juicy raisins, assorted nuts, dried figs and Christmas candies—things unattainable in our small village. It was a magic night, a night for listening for sleigh bells and reindeer hooves on the snow covered roof, for struggling to sleep lest the good Santa would find you awake and pass you by. It was a time to think of one's best ribbed stocking hanging long and thin from the hall mantle, of a tantalizing toy that would protrude from its top in the morning, of other small gifts transforming the limpness into strange lumps and bulges. One always knew that tucked in the toe would be a shiny orange, fat brown nuts and hard candy. Already the basin of water was in place near the chimney where Santa would enter, along with the usual apple, that the kind Christmas elf might wash the soot from his hands and refresh himself before leaving for some other rooftop.

It was a time for watching the firelight dance on the bedroom wall, or hearing the muted whispers of our parents as they made last minute preparations for the morning. It was a night of little sleep for them before being aroused with the excited query, "Has he been here? Is it time?" There were unrestrained shouts upon hearing them respond, "Merry Christmas!" while pulling on robes in the chilly dawn. Coals were stirred in smoldering fires; lights went on, as the five of us scrambled into clothes to descend the wide stairs. From the top landing one could see the five stuffed stockings hanging stiffly from the mantle's edge, and the shimmering tree standing guard over the array of presents.

A VIRGINIA VILLAGE

It was a time for open house on Christmas night, with blazing wood fires, the dining room table loaded with festive food. There were parties for young and old and a community tree with a real live Santa handing out bags of goodies to the children. There was the annual romp in our big attic, with all playmates invited. Here a vaguely familiar Santa, in Santa Claus head with flowing beard and a bathrobe stuffed with pillows, added to the merriment. The

climax of the fun was breaking the large paper bag suspended from the ceiling, showering nuts, candy and cakes onto the cloth below. It was the season for young girls to show off new party dresses and boys to make a special date with a special girl for the important

CHRISTMAS

Christmas dance. It was a time for visiting about the neighborhood, for informal gatherings of gown-ups in the evenings.

It was a mellow time, a time for calling out the cherry old greeting, "Christmas Gift!" to one and all, for singing carols on dusky street corners and in the dimly lit country church. It was a time for hearing again the familiar Christmas story told from the little chancel, now lovingly decorated with holiday greens and fat, red candles. It was that time when a spirit of love, of joy, of faith radiated among the people. It was the season to cherish anew those blessed gifts bestowed by Christ. It was Christmas.

A VIRGINIA VILLAGE

24
FRINGE BENEFITS

Our household never seemed complete without the presence of one or more aunts, a vital if unobtrusive addition to the family. Most especially, there was Aunt Chris, a petite, silver haired little widow who made her home with us the better part of the year, the remaining time with her son in Georgia.

Fastidious about her appearance, it took her more than average time to complete the everyday ritual of getting dressed. Each small, gray hairpin must be exactly in place, a fresh handkerchief sprinkled with toilet water in the pocket of her dress, the small string of graded pearls fastened about her neck. Finally, there was the important rite of heating her old fashioned curling irons in the flame of an oil lamp for that special last crimp in her thin white hair, formally teased into a pompadour above her serious, round face.

This unobtrusive little person was especially gifted with her needle, making her own ankle length black dresses, adding a touch of handwork to collar and cuffs. Seldom was she without some bit of sewing in her lap doing the daintiest of embroidery on center piece and mats, hemstitching linen towels, initialing linen napkins and pillow slips. There might be crocheting or knitting of soft wool bed jackets.

Simple in her faith, childlike in her reasoning, this little aunt was by nature pessimistic, wearing habitually an air of melancholy. Calamity lurked around every corner, and the wicked world was headed for destruction. This side of her personality was taken lightly by those about her, for everyone knew it was just her way. Only Papa poked fun at her air of gloom and teasingly called her "Calamity Chris."

A VIRGINIA VILLAGE

There was once a time that the Ouija Board invaded the country and many of our homes, creating for the most part skeptic amusement. Little Aunt Chris, true to nature with her naive beliefs, took it seriously, entertaining the hope she might communicate with the departed spirits in the other world, specifically her deceased husband. All sewing would be put aside if she could find someone willing to sit fingers to fingers, knee to knee, as she seriously asked questions to the inscrutable Ouija.

There were other sides to the nature of this gentle little soul, which overshadowed those things of lesser importance, and endeared her to all. Kind, generous, capable, dependable: the small figure rose to a towering height of strength in a time of emergency or need.

Ours was a clannish family, and each relative and in-law had a special corner in our affections, a special place in our lives. They were all fringe benefits, so to speak.

Married to the daughter of a judge in Savannah, the son of Aunt Chris was a lawyer of no little stature. Respected and loved in his adopted land, he maintained always an allegiance to his home state of Virginia, especially this Tidewater section where he grew up. He always said the familiar and loved ballad, "Carry Me Back To Old Virginny" never ceased to give him nostalgic yearning. Fiercely clannish, he returned happily each year to make the rounds of his Virginia relatives. Handsome, attractive, full of reminiscences of the past, filled with charming stories of the Deep South, he was always a welcome guest. The following is a delightful story he once told in his own inimitable way. It was a true story, an incident that took place in the Federal Court of Savannah, related by the presiding judge.

It seems that there was an old darkie by the name of Christmas Moultrie who had been brought into court on the charge of

FRINGE BENEFITS

shooting Summer Duck. At that time, Summer Duck, known also as Wood Duck, were protected by law. "Christmas," the judge's voice boomed, "tell the court in your own words just what happened."

> "Well sah, Jedge," the old man answered, twisting his battered hat in gnarled fingers, "I was paddlin' up dis yere slue when two ob dem Summer Ducks riz up jes head ob me, and I up wid my gun and shoot—Keboom . . . Keflooey . . . and one ob dem ducks come fallin' down daid. Den, sah, yer honor, jes bout de time I reach fer to thow hem in de boat, dat genn'mun (pointing to the Federal Agent) poke his haid from roun de bushes an say, "Uhhh huhh, Christmas, we done got you at las . . . an . . . " Here the judge interruped the old man, "Christmas," he demanded, "when you saw you had killed a Summer Duck, why didn't you drop it back in the marsh?" The old man stared at the judge incredulously, then replied, "Jedge, sah, yo' honor, ain't you done never et Summer Duck?"

For many years after Aunt Chris and others of that older generation had passed on, this relative, and son of the Northern Neck, returned annually on his habitual visits, each year a bit more portly of girth, a shade grayer about the temple, maintaining, however, the same warm, attractive personality. Somehow, he always happened to pick the very hottest spells of summer, arriving, as was his custom, with a box of Whitman's Sampler for each and every household of relatives. I can see him now on the front step, smiling, perspiring, completely oblivious that the intense summer heat was taking its toll on the box of chocolates tucked under his arm.

A VIRGINIA VILLAGE

25

WASHINGTON SLEPT HERE

The brick lodge house near the entrance gate was only one of the many things that make Sabine Hall special, that set it apart from many of the homes of that time. A delightful memory is that of the old colored gatekeeper, doffing his hat in a courtly manner as he emerged from the gatehouse to greet visitors. The driveway led through a park of fine trees to the lovely house with its classic Greek portico.

To me, there is no home in Tidewater Virginia more typically southern than Sabine Hall, a handsome house of white brick with four great columns reaching to the roof. The spacious center building is joined on each side by long one story wings, stretching across the curved end of the driveway. Surrounded by fine old trees, sunlight flickers through the foliage, forming patterns of light and shadow on the mellow facade. This is a dignified, lovely home in a charming setting. Double doors at the front entrance open in a welcome to the handsome hall with fine original paneling, graceful and delicate stairway, cherished family portraits and other fine furnishings. I can visualize a time long past when visitors from other plantations and friends from the nearby village arrived by coach and carriage to enjoy the delightful hospitality of this old house and its owners. Up the stairway in the room on the left, George Washington once stayed when a guest in the house.

The terraced gardens on the riverside of the house are a distinctive and integral part of the place. As far back as I can remember, they have been lovingly cared for by the lady of the house.

Like many old places, Sabine hall had its ghost. One story I seem to remember was when a late owner of the house was ascending the stairs one night, he was grabbed by the coattail and pulled firmly back. Laughing, he admonished his young son to stop playing games but, on looking back, found no one there. Perhaps there really are wispy figures and shadowy shapes who "let loose" at times and walk abroad to plague us humans. At any rate, such legends make for fine storytelling.

In a time long ago, when the carriage from Sabine Hall would pass our house on a Sunday morning, my mother would call, "It is time, children, for you to leave for Sunday school." The shiny vehicle, with its pair of bay horses, was driven by the illustrious owner of Sabine Hall, who was Superintendent of our Sunday school. The beauty and fascination of his lovely wife was known throughout Virginia and elsewhere. She for years had been "The Belle" of The White Sulfur, that fashionable spa which attracted many from the lowlands.

It was, however, the later generations of Sabine Hall who were more intimately woven into my life and memory, and each had a special place in my affections. How can I write of so many memories, recount so many things, or relive so many moments of pleasure I spent with them and do justice to it all!

26

THE VILLAGE CHURCH

I would never be so remiss when telling of my village as to fail to speak of the church and the important place that it occupied in the community. Much of the social life centered around the church with gatherings of one kind or another, and benefits such as silver teas, along with other pleasant means of fund raising. There were bazaars in the fall, prior to which the ladies of the church met in one house or another to make plans for that important function, their needlework interspersed with lively conversation. In spring was an annual Easter egg hunt for children; and at some time during summer came the Sunday school picnic, usually held at the river near a steamboat wharf. A small tram for collecting freight from the far end of the pier made a splendid picnic table, the delectable food from the variety of home baskets arranged on a checked cloth on its top. It was a family affair. That is to say, the entire family attended, each housewife taking special pride in preparing deviled eggs, fried chicken, salads, assorted sandwiches, tarts, cakes, and many things suited to finger licking. The boys enthusiastically went swimming in the limpid river. The girls went bathing demurely garbed in knee length wool suits, with overskirts, rubber bathing caps and shoes and long black stockings. Two small sheds on the river shore afforded convenient shelter for changing clothes.

During the summer, some churches held revival meetings,

at which time their bountiful midday meal was placed on high wooden tables beneath a spreading tree on the church grounds. Then, it was during the hot month of August that the famous camp meetings took place, one known as Marvin Grove, the other as Wharton Grove, attracting crowds throughout the Northern Neck as well as elsewhere. Family cottages were scattered about the enclosures, along with the Tabernacle, communal dining center and other special places.

This annual occasion was eagerly looked forward to, especially by those owning cottages. There, young girls would wear their prettiest frocks, and keep an expectant look out for a summer romance. Indeed, many were formed under the canopy of stately oaks, or sitting on the backbench in the Tabernacle. The following article from the Northern Neck News of 1918, reprinted later, gives a colorful and factual insight into this important happening:

> All arrangements have been made for the 42nd annual encampment at Marvin Grove Camp, which begins on Aug. 2, to continue 10 days. Rev. R. F. Gayle presiding Elder of the Rappahannock District, will be in charge of the religious exercises, and the preaching will be done by Revs. W. E. Thompson of Richmond and Rev. John C. Smith, of Baltimore. The same song books which were so popular at the last meeting will be used again this year. If you have one, bring it to Camp with you, as well as your Billy Sunday Song Book.
>
> The public generally is most cordially invited to attend.
>
> Owners of cottages are urged to get their cottages in repair, and when it is possible to have the buildings white-washed.

THE VILLAGE CHURCH

Persons coming by steamer should land at Coan or Morattico. Have mail sent to Rainswood, Va.

Committee

- *Northern Neck News*, August 2, 1918
Reprint 10/5/1972, pg. 14, "Twice Told Tales"

To me, there has always been something meaningful in the sound of bells. Resonant, hollow bells, tinkling bells, pealing bells. Edgar Allen Poe, in his poem "The Bells," caught this rhythm of sound. Once in an old town in Germany, nestled in the hills of the Black Forest, I awakened on a Sunday morning to the joyful ringing of bells, their syncopated tones bouncing from the hilltops, resounding through the valley. In colonial times, the "Town Crier" would ring a bell in the streets to herald important events, and with us in our rural community, the church bell afforded a like function. It was a joyful, prolonged ringing from its small belfry that brought the glad news of the Armistice of World War I, and there was the urgent, frenzied ringing that struck fear to the heart, for the bell was also rung to warn of a fire. Able-bodied men would form a bucket brigade to the nearest well, sometimes saving the burning buildings. Then there was the melancholy, solemn tolling that noted the burial of the dead. But, more especially, the church bell rang to break the silence of the Sabbath morning, with an invitation to worship. "Hurry, children. The bell for Sunday school just rang." Dressed in Sunday clothes, we took the narrow, dirt sidewalk through the village and over the slight hill. Little girls wore long-waisted muslin dresses, with ribbon sash and pinned with beauty pins, bonnets trimmed with forget-me-nots. Small boys wore knee pants, white blouse and Windsor tie. Clutched in a moist hand was a five-cent piece for collection. During the Lenten

Season, each had his own Mite Box, turned in on Easter morning, the loose change earned by doing home chores or odd jobs about the neighborhood.

It was in the little ivy-covered church with yellow brick columns and a bell tower that I felt I belonged. There the tall Gothic windows with clear glass panes brought in the out of doors: sunlight that danced on the old marble font and red carpet, and cast a band of gold across steps of the small chancel. Through an open window, waving green tree branches were lively against a pale sky. Once I heard a bird sing joyously from a top bough, seemingly vying with the voice of the minister and the defensive rustle of paper fans against summer's heat.

To the back of the chancel was a stained glass window, and to the side, a modest choir stall with old-fashioned pedal-pumped organ. There were no choir vestments, for there was no regular choir, as choirs go. Rather, it was composed of anyone, of any age, who happened to be at church and could "turn a tune." For that reason, it might seem odd that Miss Coley was known as the choir leader. A dainty little person, she would usually arrive quite

THE VILLAGE CHURCH

breathless, and almost late, with hymnbook tucked under her arm. I can remember her in the front pew of the choir, patting her small foot, keeping time, her true, if thin, soprano taking the lead. Outside the church, carriages and buggies sat empty, the horses tied to a convenient post or tree limb. They waited patiently, nodding in the morning sun. Inside, there was a dignity without stiffness, respect without awe, serenity without apathy in the inviting quiet of the little church: a feeling of belonging.

A VIRGINIA VILLAGE

27

THE JUDGE

Wilna, the attractive old brick house surrounded by broad fields and bordered on one side by the Rappahannock River, was Papa's boyhood home. Built by my great grandfather, this house had many attractive features that remain today, including old pine floors, mantles and paneling. A narrow stairway led to two bedrooms on the top floor of this three story house, formerly the bedrooms of my father and his two younger brothers. From one of the windows, the little boys communicated by signals to their friends in the village on the opposite shore. It's been said that from this same window my great grandmother once waved her ruffled petticoat, a prearranged signal for needed assistance. It was, in this case, a small fire in an outbuilding.

Papa was only eight when his mother died, but he keenly remembered that cold winter's morning. How unreal seemed the familiar reflection of firelight on the plastered bedroom walls. The numbness of reality was brought into clear focus when they advised him that, as the oldest of the little boys, he must now become a man. Feeling that responsibility, he soon began farm chores and chores about the house. Thus at an early age he was forced to grow up.

My grandfather, known to us as "Grand," was an aristocratic, courtly old gentleman—a remnant of the South before the Civil War. He had never worked with his hands, albeit there was little money and a dearth of farm help. He was now too old to change. His white hair curled over the collar of his well cut but worn broadcloth suit, and from an upper pocket his linen handkerchief emitted a faint fragrance of eau de cologne. A graduate in law, he was also a student of the classics, frequently quoting Ovid or Virgil as he rocked leisurely on his long veranda.

A time came when the two younger boys could take over the responsibility relegated to my father, and Papa broke from home ties, securing a position as tutor in a private home in South Carolina. It was there he said he learned to like ham hock and grits. Reading law at night, he eventually managed some time at The University, passed the bar examination, and finally took up law practice in the little village he was to make his home. Knowledgeable and ambitious, the young lawyer soon won the respect and fondness of those around him. "Let's take up collection and get Joe a haircut," chided an older lawyer and friend. But, it was of no matter to Papa that his dark hair hung over his collar, for haircut money at that time was hard to come by, and there were more important needs. Success was within his grasp, and it was not long before he became Commonwealth's Attorney at the age of twenty-three. Recognized for his knowledge of law, his sense of justice and keen perception, he was soon elevated to the Circuit Bench.

Once Papa joined some men on a trip overseas, and on his return his baggage bulged with gifts and mementos from places he had visited. "There is," he quietly said when the excitement of "gift opening" had died down, "something I had shipped from Italy, but for the life of me I cannot remember what . . . " adding "I believe it must be marble." "I hope it is a birdbath," Mama exclaimed. Before notice of its arrival, Papa vowed he did not believe he would bother to claim or pay duty on whatever it was, and it was Mama who insisted. It was not a birdbath. It was two pieces of marble statuary: the Crouching Venus, and the Discus Thrower. Though quite lovely, there was a question as to where to put such works of art, befitting some formal garden or gallery. The

THE JUDGE

Crouching Venus finally rested on the pier table in our parlor. The graceful Discus Thrower, as I recall, stood some years on its green marble base in our side porch. Today, I wonder what became of them.

Everyone has his own remembrances, and the following anecdotes belong to my special picture memories. After Mama died, the big front bedroom was spoken of as "Papa's room." Beside the big carved walnut bed, a small table held an assortment of simple medicinal remedies, and at bedtime might be added a cup of hot Ovaltine, and always a small glass of "toddy" for wakeful night hours. A noticeable confusion of stains from the rims of many glasses marked the top of the small mahogany table.

But, it was the cavernous old wardrobe in Papa's bedroom that has for me a special memory. It was during days of prohibition, stills, and "moonshine" liquor that I conceived the idea I would attempt to make what was then called "home brew." I had heard that it was being done and, for that matter, there was a recipe I cut from a magazine that told how to do it. It would be my surprise for Papa. I do not know why I chose the inner recesses of Papa's wardrobe to hide the crock and its contents for the duration—that is, while it brewed. There were some days I forgot it, and days also when I made a tour of inspection. One time the pungent odor was evident upon opening the wardrobe door, and it was this that led to discovery. I did not know that Papa was close at hand. "What is this?" he wanted to know, peering over my shoulder. "I'm making some home brew," I said somewhat hesitatingly. The old gentleman looked incredulous, then amused. "Perhaps you had better remove it elsewhere, or even better, get rid of it," he said quietly. So ended a twelve-year old girl's venture into the art of "bootlegging."

As he grew older, Papa became more and more absentminded.

A VIRGINIA VILLAGE

Once, while driving in a nearby city, he was stopped by a traffic officer for not having the newly issued license plates on his small coupe. The old gentleman silently considered the matter; then, with a look of recollection, he said in his forthright way, "I remember now. I am sure I put them on the piano at home." Subsequently, that city's newspaper carried the following news item: "Judge fined for putting license plates on piano instead of car."

In his late years, Papa had a way of exercising by walking up and down our lane. At the far end was the garage, and I never seemed to back the old Buick out without slamming into the power pole on the opposite side. Somehow he never seemed to notice, but ultimately it was bound to happen. On that day, hearing the thud, he turned and slowly retraced his steps, as I awaited his reprimand. Leaning on his cane, he looked long at the offending pole, and then at me. Finally he said with a flickering smile, "It seems as though I will have to move that pole."

What I remember most particularly about Papa was his great sense of justice in all matters, big and small. Beneath his reserve was a warm sense of humor and a great generosity. His excellence as a judge on the Circuit Court, the great esteem in which he was held, and his innate honor won for him his seat on the Virginia Supreme Court.

There were special notices on radio broadcasts when he died. There were editorials in newspapers, both within and out of the state. There were letters, many letters from friends and acquaintances, to say nothing of those who knew him only by reputation. Today, the clarity of his opinions and brilliant interpretations of the law remain forever a guide for those who follow. This is the legacy he left.

28
COURT DAYS

Four of the five counties of the Northern Neck, along with Essex County to the west of the Rappahannock River, made up the judicial circuit over which my father presided. At that time, the only means of reaching the Essex side was by way of a ferryboat, piloted by old Zack, a well known character in these parts. When in need of passage, should the ferryboat be on the opposite shore, it was necessary to hoist a white flag, then await Zack's convenience. There was a time when one's patience was sorely tried, but good humor was restored when he finally arrived, white teeth flashing in a smiling face. When the town of Tappahannock was their destination, because of the proximity to the ferry landing, passengers from the Northern Neck left cars on their home side.

My father related a story about one time when he crossed on the ferry to hold a day's session of court, accompanied by several businessmen from the village on missions of their own. It had been a long and tiresome day when they assembled at the small landing to head for home on Zack's ferry. Once on board, someone produced a bottle and, seemingly, no one was averse to a little "swallow" to allay the pangs of fatigue, even "Seldom Drinker" and "Avowed Abstainer." Midway the river, threatening black clouds in the west gathered into a storm. Thunder rolled, lightening flashed and wind blew a gale, followed by torrential rain. Without a car, they were without shelter on the flat bottom open boat, which pitched and tossed in the choppy river. Zack's white teeth no longer smiled as he lent his energy to keeping the boat on a straight course for the other shore. Papa, who had no fear of water or storms, once reconciled to the drenching he was getting, gave over to enjoying the experience—that is, until he took note of his fellow companions. "Seldom Drinker," a yellowish green, was sick over the low rail. The rest, a small, miserable group, huddled in the center of the pitching boat. Water poured from the drooping brims of their hats, ran in rivulets down upturned collars, and streamed from their coat tails as the wind wrapped sodden pants about their unsteady legs. With a pale, strained face, "Avowed Abstainer" dropped to his knees on the rolling deck. Right then he fervently prayed aloud for the Lord's forgiveness for that "one swallow." "I thought I was a 'goner," he later confessed.

When the county court was in session, the small country hotels and inns were filled, straining their modest accommodations. For the most part, there was a dearth of transients, except for the usual drummers on routine visits to country merchants, their black satchels filled with samples from some factory outlet. Occasionally there was a permanent boarder such as a local bachelor, and sometimes a teacher from away, who lived there during the school months. A brick terrace alongside our village hotel led to the office of the owner-proprietor. There, great hickory logs in an open fireplace burned consistently through winter months. The glowing coals massed below supporting andirons left a mound of gray ashes throughout the summer. It was a simple room, portraying the personality of the owner, a rugged man with silvery white hair, stiff moustache and faithful corncob

COURT DAYS

pipe. An avid hunter and fisherman, the walls displayed

WALLACE HOTEL

trophies of his take. A shotgun stood in the chimney corner, and an old red setter slept and dreamed before the fire. When the bell in the latticed cupola outside rang the hour of twelve, it was a call to midday dinner in the plain dining room, where the cotton cloths on the long tables were covered by a protective oilcloth. Guests of the hotel ate family style, passing dishes of food up one side, down the other, in a friendly good humor. Mid-center the table, a bottle of catsup towered over a squat sugar bowl, while along the sides marched thick water glasses. From under the kitchen door seeped the odor of boiled cabbage, turnip greens and other indications of the coming meal.

A dirt sidewalk and road ran past the sloping banks of our front yard, where a white board fence formed the boundary for us five children. Outside the fence was always prohibited during March court, when the village thronged with a pouring-in from the countryside. March court was a time for horse trading and showing of sleek stallions, harnessed to small sulkies. Like black birds, we lined the top rail of the fence to watch horses and drivers pass down the dusty road. Inside the stolid courthouse, the proceedings of law and justice carried on, while on the courthouse green a spirit of conviviality prevailed, a lighter mood of handshaking, of greeting old friends and exchanging pleasantries. It's been said that many business deals were consummated in the shade of the big oaks.

The interiors of most courthouses that I am familiar with have more or less the same arrangement. The flag of the Commonwealth of Virginia on one side of the judge's stand, the American flag on the other. Like positions are occupied by steel engravings of the two beloved Confederate generals, Robert E. Lee and Stonewall Jackson. The space above the judge's stand is usually reserved for, or filled with, a portrait of some distinguished local jurist. Marble tablets, with names of past prominent officials, as well as others listing local war dead, hang on the side walls, along with portraits of other outstanding members of the bar.

Court day found our kitchen stove filled with pots and kettles of various sizes, for my mother would say, "Your father will most certainly be bringing someone home for midday dinner." It could be a lawyer and friend, "Cap'n Billie," maybe Mr. Norris—a courtly barrister of the Northern Neck—maybe our friend, "The Colonel," maybe all three, or it could be Mr. Jim C., the tenant from our small farm down the road. Mr. Jim came twice a year to "settle up."

COURT DAYS

I can remember his taking from various pockets in his suit small tobacco bags containing wads of soiled bills, as well as coin of all denominations. Though Mr. Jim could neither read nor write, there was never an error, so accurate was his memory. There was never need for the detailed, much folded memorandum furnished by his school-aged son. Kindness and honesty marked his weathered face; laughter wrinkles creased the corners of his light blue eyes, filled with candor and trust. Though he always protested "I ain't hungry," with some coaxing he usually came to the table. On one memorable day, he was accompanied by his four-year-old granddaughter. I cannot forget that, in answer to my mother's query, we learned from Mr. Jim that her name was Queen Victoria. With us children there was a moment of suppressed mirth, kept well in check by my mother. Queen Victoria was treated with all the dignity her name suggested, and right then the old highchair, long relegated to the dining room closet, was brought out and placed by my mother's elbow. The golden-haired, blue-eyed "Queen" unconcerned, obviously happy, mounted her throne.

A VIRGINIA VILLAGE

29

THE GIRLS

It seems superfluous for me to attempt to describe any of the handsome old homes in this area, for this has been done many times by distinguished architects and historians. There has already been so much written about the following place by knowledgeable persons, it is most unlikely I can add anything other than a few personal recollections. Following, however, is a brief description.

Stately, lovely Mt. Airy rests on a promontory surrounded by vast acres, with a distant view of the Rappahannock River. The house, of massive construction, is of native brown sandstone, and attached to the great center building are curved wings, or passageways, leading to the dependencies. A distinctive feature might well be two great iron dogs standing guard upon the walls on each side of the steps to the high porch. Built in 1758, Mt. Airy still remains in the family of the original builder and owner. In 1884, the main house was gutted by a fire which changed somewhat the interior—specifically the stairway—and I have heard the wooden floors in the great hall were once of marble. It is interesting to note that, following this fire, the bedroom doors were replaced with doors brought from the old Willard Hotel in Washington, D.C., which was then being remodeled.

To the west of the mansion was the bowling green, surrounded by rose borders, and on the next level, flowering shrubs edged a wide gravel walkway. Low fruit bushes defined the last terrace, where one looked down upon the "flats" and what was once their private racetrack. The library walls in the big house displayed many interesting pictures of fine racehorses from the stables at Mt. Airy.

A VIRGINIA VILLAGE

Here I must mention the walkway of English Box leading to what remained of the orangery, a type of hot house rarely seen in this area of Virginia. A delightful little anecdote they told at Mt. Airy pertained to a winter's day when General Lafayette once visited there. Though the ground was covered with snow, such as a Virginia winter might bring, they offered their distinguished guest fresh, ripe strawberries from the orangery, along with rich country cream from their own dairy house.

As handsome as it is, I have always felt this great, formal house would be cold were it not for the gentle, hospitable owners. Embracing a host of relatives and friends, the three gracious sisters lent warmth and charm to the halls of Mt. Airy. To us they were more than relatives, for devotion extended far beyond family ties.

Among my countless memories, I recall that some of us children spent several weeks with them to escape the nearness of the virulent flu of the 1917 epidemic. There we had endless new and exciting things to do, like rolling down terraces on the lawn, playing in the wonderful old, dark barn, and climbing trees in the extensive deer park that reaches to the far end of their driveway. In the familiar hall of the big house, there was the ancient hand organ, or music box, with huge spiked cylinders, which we never tired of playing. Then, too, we never tired of hearing the exciting story of when the Yankee soldiers came to Mt. Airy. As one of these men turned the handle on the old organ, just by chance it played the well-known tune, "Yankee Doodle." Some local citizens have surmised that this may have been the reason the handsome house was not molested during the war.

The sisters had their own special way of "making do," of giving simple things a touch of the exotic. Such was the everyday meal in the dining room, where ancestral portraits looked down from the side walls onto the daintily set table with its simple

THE GIRLS

repast: a cold meat, watermelon pickle in a cut glass dish near the hand-embroidered centerpiece, baked egg plant, homemade rolls in the warming oven, now pulled close to the table. It all took on a festive air, especially if there was their special kind of caramel ice cream, "turned out" on a flowered platter with the familiar heavy silver serving spoon. I recall, too, many afternoon teas in the big hall, with crullers, cheese macaroons, their own dandelion wine, and perhaps their special liqueur made from crushed rose petals.

In those days, few, if any, country places had central heat. After supper, we gathered about the wood stove in the big, shadowy hall. There in the lamplight, two sisters did embroidery, or some other form of handwork, while the third sister read aloud to us children. Eventually came time to climb the winding stairs to the dimly lit upper hall, to the warmth of the inviting bedroom in soft lamplight. In footed pajamas, we knelt in a row by the high bed that they might hear our prayers.

These are just a few among the avalanche of memories to do with these favorite relatives. Yes, they had their own special place in the affections of our family.

It would not have seemed right at Christmas—more especially Christmas night—for these special cousins not to be at our house. There was one time, however, when it looked to be impossible. For two days, a heavy snow had fallen, drifts piling high in unsuspected places, roadways and fields an expanse of untrammeled white. They called to say their long lane was impassable: they were snowbound. This news cast a shadow of disappointment over the festive preparations, albeit the fire blazed merrily in our front hall, the ornaments on the Christmas tree nearby reflecting the dancing flames. The day was waning, dusk descending on the countryside. Soon those from around the village would arrive for our annual "open house." My mother was seeing

A VIRGINIA VILLAGE

to the placing of holiday food on the long dining room table when there was a commotion on the front porch. "Christmas Gift!" came familiar voices as they pushed open the front door, bringing in a rush of cold air and a sprinkling of snow on their coats and mufflers. They held gaily-tied packages of homemade orange peel, and pecan nuts from their own trees.

"Christmas Gift! . . . Christmas Gift!" they repeated, kissed each one around, their eyes sparkling with excitement, their cheeks stiff from the cold. "However did you get here?" my mother asked, as she delightedly hurried to meet them. They had walked the two

or three miles. Such was the will and undaunted spirit of these very special people. It was only their driveway that was closed. Later, my father drove them back to their own white gate at the entrance to their lane, and walked with them to the dark and stolid old house, framed in a background of white.

30

ENTERTAINMENT

There was always a wave of excitement in most rural areas when an itinerant show, complete with tent, a knocked down platform and portable gas lamps, set up on some vacant lot on the fringe of the village. Known as the Medicine Show, it lured many to its free entertainment, with the ultimate intent of selling the captive audience its fake medicine. The gathering of spectators watched spellbound the sad eyed magician in a straw "skimmer," a flashing stickpin in his flowered cravat, pull a rabbit from a hat or a string of colored scarfs from his coat sleeve. Dyed yellow hair piled high above swinging ear pendants, and hands ablaze with paste diamonds, his blowsy helper pirouetted about the crude stage, the sequins on her tawdry dress shimmering in the flickering lamp light. The third member of the little cast was the Medicine Man himself: tall, sallow, in a rusted frock coat, string tie and black fedora. His uncertain talent, it seemed, was a running commentary on the merits of "Pain King." This wonder drug, he convinced his audience, was a cure all for every ill . . . warts, indigestion, in growing toenails, baldness, water on the knee . . . he named many more while the brown liquid was being dispersed at fifty cents a bottle. A time came when this type of show was proclaimed a fraud, a means of flimflamming the public, so the arm of the law reached out and the Medicine Man came to an end. In its place came the traveling carnival, complete with merry-go-round, miniature roller coaster and like amusements.

Once, home theatricals were a means of fun and amusement. Although it would be frowned upon today, in most villages the courthouse was the largest public building and, out of necessity, it was used for things other than dealing with justice. It necessitated careful planning ahead as to available time between legal schedules. I recall once a minstrel show, with the end men in black face and white gloves, enjoying their spot in the limelight, with songs almost risqué, jokes a bit off color. There was always excited speculation by the home audience in the crowded room as to "who was who," and childlike pleasure when recognizing a familiar face behind the grease paint. There is nothing like the rapport between player and audience in a display of home talent.

The very first moving picture to come our way was projected on a sheet stretched taut on the back wall of the courthouse. In retrospect, there was not much coherence, but it was spellbinding, with Lilliputian figures, images of real people moving in jerky motion across the improvised screen. There were no captions to relate what the voiceless lips were saying. Rather, the one responsible for bringing us this miracle told or read the story as it unfolded. Our first and last movie house some years later was plain and unattractive, but it brought to our community the spectacular new form of entertainment of a fast growing enterprise. This was all about the time when Rudolph Valentino, darkly handsome in the white robe of The Sheik, streaked about the desert on an Arabian horse, carrying the swooning heroine to his tent beneath the stars. There was popular swash buckling Douglas Fairbanks, becoming even more sensational when he married "America's Sweetheart," Mary Pickford. I remember the Gish Sisters in "Way Down East," Clara Bow, the "It Girl," Charlie Chaplin, Laurel and Hardy, to name a few from that magnetic world of entertainment. They flashed across the screen in our small primitive movie theater, with its hard seats and background music from a windup Victrola.

ENTERTAINMENT

"Come to the fair," the country fair, that is, with the selected displays of grain and other produce from local farms. Here one found pens of livestock, bedded knee-deep in yellow straw, coops of poultry of all kinds, horses, cows, mules, goats and hogs: everything one associates with a farm and the hard working farmer. Not to be overlooked is the farmer's wife, whose day began at the break of dawn, feeding the men and getting them off to the fields. She then faced her daily chores of churning, tending the poultry, cooking, cleaning, mending, canning and preserving. Lastly, time must be set aside to work on exhibits for the annual fall fair . . . a crocheted bedspread, a special jar of cucumber pickle, or a cross-stitched sampler. Then, under a September sun, the midway came alive with a Ferris wheel, merry-go-round, barkers, concession stands, hot dogs, booths, tinseled Cupid dolls, cotton candy, dust and heat. But above all, it was an agricultural fair, and it belonged to the farmer and the people. For the farmer's wife, there was no little pride in the blue ribbon about her jar of special pickle.

There was a feel of spring in the air, also a feeling of excitement. Adults came from living room and kitchen to surrounding yards, and children once again lined the top rail of the fence, for it was generally known the circus parade would pass this way. The thrilling, once-a-year circus was back. Tompkins' Wild West Show, it was called, and all ages were drawn to the spectacle of the parade and the show that followed in the big tent. In the distance, one heard the organ-like sound of the calliope, a forerunner of the circus band, and then there came circus wagons with life-like pictures of wild animals on the sides. Behind the gilded bars were real animals: a snarling lion, a hairy gorilla, beady-eyed monkeys, many frightening, beautiful creatures—like your animal picture book come alive. There was a striped zebra, a moth-eaten camel

A VIRGINIA VILLAGE

and lovely white horses, red pom-poms in their bridles, and spangled circus girls on their backs. Like the three bears, always there were three elephants that returned each year. They lumbered by on huge feet, the second and third holding the tail of the one in

front. They were always a favorite.

In a field of stubble, out from the village, loomed the big tent, its canvas stretched taut over the cavernous interior. Sawdust, popcorn, animal flesh—the smell of the circus was in the air. Sitting on the bottom row of the bleachers, I watched, spellbound, animal acts, acrobats and clowns performing in the ring in front of me, and I gazed with awe at the artist in spangled pink tights high above. She was Flossie Tompkins, the pretty daughter of the circus owner, the star attraction who was performing high in the arch of the tent. Swinging from a trapeze, sailing lightly through the air, she was caught by her male companion hanging adroitly from the bar of his trapeze. There was an audible gasp of relief from the large crowd when the act was safely consummated. Finally, hanging by her teeth, she spun a dazzling whirl of pink and silver. The return of Tompkins' Wild West Show each year meant also

ENTERTAINMENT

the return of Flossie Tompkins, the darling of the circus, whom the little village had taken to its heart.

By far the most elevating, the most erudite entertainment to come our way was the Radcliffe Chautauqua, sponsored by a group of local citizens. Home schedules went awry that special week of summer, for those with season tickets must hurry home from the matinee for supper to "freshen up" for the night performance. It was usually August when the Chautauqua came, with the hot afternoon sun beating down on canvas tent, housing both players and audience. Summer clothes would stick to the rough, wooden benches, and the performers constantly swabbed their streaming faces. Eventually, someone took things in hand and rolled up the side flaps of the tent to any air that might find its way inside. My mother, in a very damp, sheer voile, fanned happily with a large palm leaf fan.

Crammed with varied forms of entertainment, it had something to appeal to everyone. Block or season tickets, sold in advance, entitled the holder to both matinee and evening performances, completing a schedule of variable and pleasant entertainment. A portly, blond soprano sang such familiar ballads as "Kreisler's Old Refrain," the "Lohengrin Song," and "From the Land of the Sky Blue Waters," with appropriate encores. She was a favorite with my mother. I remember a pianist whose fingers fairly danced over the keys in "Flight of the Bumble Bee." Or she might render the lovely "Moonlight Sonata." Comedies, skits, pantomime, acrobatics, juggling—even one-act plays—made up the daily schedules. Adults, especially, looked forward to speakers from some well-known seat of learning, or other places of importance, who lent an erudite touch to the prevailing lighter mood. The following is taken from a 1918 edition of the *Northern Neck News*, reprinted later in the column, "Twice Told Tales":

A VIRGINIA VILLAGE

> Radcliffe Chautauqua which exhibited here on Friday, Saturday and Monday last, was largely attended and greatly enjoyed. Crowds came from miles around, and the closing night, Dr. R. W. Moore, President of Colgate University, N. Y., spoke to an appreciative audience, subject, "He Took It Upon Himself." . . . There being about 30 guaranteers. Something over $25.00 was realized above expenses. Through the courtesy of Mr. Harry Arnest, agent for the Delco Lighting System, the tent was brilliantly lighted with electric lights each night.
>
> —*Northern Neck News*, July 19, 1918
> Reprint 10/19/1972, "Twice told tales"

In the final analysis of all the entertainment, this was bound to be the most anticipated, the most delightful, the most alluring, and certainly the most unique: the showboat, known as Adams Floating Theater. This picturesque form of houseboat, with name emblazoned on its side, brought the first live theater to the hamlets and villages bordering the wide rivers. Wherever and whenever it tied its lines, made fast its anchor, it attracted the entire countryside. For that matter, so great was its fame, they came from the distant cities to board its gangplank for an evening of rare pleasure in an unusual setting. The following insert from the *Northern Neck News* gives the history of the unusual type of show business:

SHOWBOAT WILL BE ON VIRGINIA RIVERS

> "The Adams Floating Theatre," one of the original "show boats" celebrated on the screen, stage and in story, will be on the Potomac and Rappahannock rivers this summer. Large numbers of Richmonders are expected to motor to Tappahannock, Kilmarnock, or Bundicks when the show boat plays at these cities.
>
> Edna Ferber, although she has prefaced her book with an explanation that it is all fiction, spent some time aboard the Adams Floating Theatre in writing her novel of such boats on the Mississippi. The theatre seats 750 persons in its boxes, orchestra and balcony. It carries its own floating

ENTERTAINMENT

lighthouse, and is equipped with dressing rooms, sleeping quarters, dining rooms and kitchen.

There is a nightly change of bill and the floating company pays (sic.) to capacity houses. Among the offerings are "Kentucky Sue", "Why Girls Walk Home", "The Rose of Mexico," and "The Broken Butterfly."

—Northern Neck News, May 31, 1929
Reprint 10/24/1974, pg. 21.

The inside of this floating structure was indeed the facsimile of a theater with elevated seats, a stage with red velvet curtains and walls of blue and gold designs. The sounds of a lively little band greeted one at the gangplank. With afternoon and night performances, the enduring cast played always to a packed house, with well-acted, well-staged plays, albeit they were simple and unsophisticated. The enthusiastic audience nearly—but not quite—hissed the villain and wept for Little Nell in "Ten Nights in a Bar-room." It was Beulah Adams, like Flossie Tompkins of the circus, who became the darling of the floating theater. Returning each season, with one more year added to her dubious age, she still played the part of the soubrette with remarkable freshness and appeal. It was a sentimental age when the onlooker lived the romance of the sweet young thing and her handsome lover. The audience sat, adoring, through "Rebecca of Sunnybrook Farm," "The Trail of the Lonesome Pine," and other endearing types of soap opera. The boat, secured to a convenient wharf or pier, its lights twinkling like jewels in the soft darkness of a country night, radiated an air of gaiety, an aura of glamour, of dreams of far off unknown places. More realistically, it gave promise of the pleasure at hand.

There is nostalgia about those simple days of the past. There is a desire to return once more to those halcyon days, to the time when the Floating Theater came our way.

A VIRGINIA VILLAGE

31

THE COLONEL

He was called Senator or Colonel, this prominent lawyer and member of the State Senate. I seem to remember him in a Palm Beach suit with a black bow tie, his full, florid face shaded by a brimmed Panama, the familiar cane supporting his portly weight. An imposing speaker, whether addressing a jury or delivering a speech from the floor of the Senate, he enjoyed a wide reputation for his wit, his humor, for his extensive vocabulary and colorful use of words. This reputation gained for him the esteemed title of "The Silver Tongued Orator."

My father's friend of long standing, the Colonel was often a delightful guest in our house. I can picture those evenings, with supper over and mama at the piano, when he led us five children in spirited singing: "Captain Jinx of the Horse Marine," "Yellow Rose of Texas," "Clementine."

A VIRGINIA VILLAGE

The fish story, as it was known, gained wide publicity in and around the Northern Neck. It had to do with a simple meal at our house, a rockfish, and our friend, the Colonel. It was during World War I, and Papa, like countless others, was concerned no little bit over the rising cost of living. At the dinner table, carving knife suspended in mid-air, he dealt at great length on this profound subject. "The cost of everything is out of all reason, Tom. Now take this fish . . . . Not too many weeks ago, it would cost about twenty-five cents; now, today, it has doubled." Listening intently, the Colonel nodded in meaningful agreement, and Papa returned to the task at hand. "Now, Tom, let me help you," he said. With a solemn expression, belying the twinkle in his eyes, the Colonel passed his plate. "Just ten cents worth, please."

My mother, as was often her lot, was at this particular time in the process of training a new maid, a tall mulatto, whose high cheekbones bore evidence of her Indian background. That evening, the old Colonel would be having dinner with us, and in the last minute of final preparation, my mother admonished Alice to be sure and change her uniform before serving dinner. We had already entered the dining room, and with our guest, were seated expectantly about the big table. In answer to my mother's summons via the bell under the table, Alice appeared in the doorway. There was a profound silence, as everyone stared in amused disbelief. She wore a black lace evening dress, with scooped neckline and dipping hem above well-worn tennis shoes. About her head was tied a cerise velvet ribbon which held a large breast pin mid-center her forehead. "Miss Sally," she asked with frigid dignity, "Miss Sally, did you blow?" Regaining her composure, my mother told her to bring in the platter of roast beef. "It seems to me," said the Colonel, when the door had closed behind her, "we should feel greatly honored. It is not often one is

THE COLONEL

served by the Queen of Sheba." There was relaxed laughter and normal conversation, while the tall Alice, unabashed, continued to serve in all her finery.

There were many stories woven around Colonel Downing, but one I like to remember was on the occasion when the bridge that bears his name was dedicated. It was an event of great importance, with a gathering of dignitaries and throngs of people from all around the state. Along with the cutting of ribbons, oratory was the order of the day, with many flowery allusions to the exciting new bridge spanning the Rappahannock River.

The following is not in anyway supposed to be a replica of those orations, now lost in obscurity. Rather, they are written in my words, in an attempt to portray with some recollection of fact the mood of good-natured jest and flattery, sometimes verbose oratory. Following is the gist of the opening address by Senator Wright, an impressive speaker from the south side of the river:

> Distinguished guests, ladies and gentlemen, we gather today on this unprecedented and historic occasion to dedicate this magnificent span which connects the shores of the Southside with those of the Northern Neck. It stands finally a symbol of progress, a tribute of ingenuity of man, the culmination of a dream that took seed in the minds and hearts of a people. At long last an ambition is realized, bringing important changes to all, especially to those of the Northern Neck, that remote peninsula set apart from the mainstream of life. Today marks for them an end to this isolation, their frustrated desires, and thwarted ambitions. No longer need they wear the cloak of obscurity. Rather, they bask now in the light of new opportunity and breathe the sweet air of freedom as they stand on the threshold of a new horizon. Today they are emancipated. It seems altogether fitting that we of the Southside be united with our neighbors across the way; for here, in this famous tidewater section, where our nation had its beginnings, there exists between us a bond of historic significance--the background of a common heritage, the inherent virtues of a stalwart peoples. Our early forefathers, born of English ancestry, endured like hardships, survived like perils, and shared common roots. Today, I deem it a privilege to extend to those neighbors and friends a sincere welcome to our shores,

A VIRGINIA VILLAGE

and wish them God Speed, as they set out on the new highway of freedom.

It was time now for the old Colonel to speak. Then it was that a favorite son of the Northern Neck, the "Silver Tongued Orator," took up the challenge:

> My friends, my countrymen, distinguished guests . . . .We, of this seemingly benighted land, the great Northern Neck, humbly appreciate the words of wisdom from the worthy Senator from across the pond. We are duly impressed by his solicitude for our years of unenlightenment. The distinguished Senator is, however, in error. Never have we worn the cloak of obscurity, but rather a shining mantle of pride in our famous forefathers who laid the foundation upon which our country rests. We do not bask purely in the light of our many great sons of history, but also in the light of our many great who followed. It is not for us to live solely in the reflected glory of the past, for as it is elegantly expressed in the following lines from Longfellow's immortal poem:
>
>> "Lives of great men all remind us
>> We should make our lives sublime
>> And departing leave behind us
>> Footprints in the sands of time."
>
> We offer no apology for our isolated land, a *garden spot of Virginia*, endowed by nature's finest gifts, settled by early land owners of stalwart fortitude. Christian in faith and love for fellowmen, we are most assuredly counted among God's chosen few.
>
> It is true that today we are emancipated, but happily not rid of the bonds that bind us forever to our hallowed land. 'Tis true today hordes are crossing this great span that links our pristine shores with the mundane outside. Yes, 'tis the very birds of the air are winging their way across the skies. The lowly muskrat, forsaking home marshes, swims out to stream. Indeed, all living creatures are heading for that unknown shore. But . . . my friends . . . when the evening sun sets behind distant rooftops and the twilight slips into the dusk of approaching night, they will return. The same birds will fly back eagerly to home nests; the muskrat seek again his humble abode. Those same hordes who crossed over to the other side will turn East--to home.

THE COLONEL

Then . . . if you listen closely, you will hear them singing in happy accord . . . "Home Sweet Home."

I was in my late teens when he died, my father's old friend, and felt honored that they gave me the opportunity of having a try at painting his portrait for the courthouse in his village. I felt it a compliment when one of his contemporaries on seeing the painting said, "That's him, all right . . . That's the Colonel," adding with a twinkle, "I can 'most smell the whiskey on his breath."

He must have been truly a colorful personality for me to remember him so vividly.

A VIRGINIA VILLAGE

CONCLUSION

Time does not stand still, and there is evidence of growth, of change in the physical aspects of the village—new homes, new peoples, and new enterprise. Caught up in the evolution of progress, the big country house, so much a part of my past, is too large to conform to family life as we know it today. It now portrays a different image, a new meaning to those in the community and about this Tidewater area, for it stands today dignified, impressive—the nucleus of a college.

The sunny nursery and its memories of early childhood, the big kitchen, once the heart of a home, the dining room where French doors led to a much used porch, the sitting room and all the rest have given way to modern classrooms or offices. The massive front door that opened to the big hall opens now to new horizons. A sloping green lawn, once framed by a white board fence for retaining carefree children, contains now serious young students. The beloved old walnut tree, that long spread its arms in welcome at the corner of our lane, has given way to an institution, welcoming students on their journey to self-realization.

It was not perfect, this village. It had its share of joys and sorrows, of highlights and shadows, as the passage of time rolled over it. It was a normal people in a normal community, and with the inevitable loss of its elderly, there were new lives to take their places. While there was gossip and prejudice, so also was there friendship and love. There was no sophisticated society, no special glamour, no wealth in this village. Deep in Tidewater Virginia, fifty miles from a railroad, life was enriching and enduring, for the bonds of friendship transcended trivialities. Thoughts crowd one another as my mind slips into the past, bringing remembered scenes and mixed emotions.

A VIRGINIA VILLAGE

Did you ever walk down a village road on a late summer evening, the smoky darkness lighted only by a canopy of stars, or on a winter's night, with only the white of newly fallen snow to help show the way? Then you must have some time known the loneliness, the yearning that at times envelops a village. How friendly, yet how distant, shone the infrequent lights from square yellow panes! How far one's voice carried in the silent stillness, when the sounds of day withdrew into the night. Such was this village, on the threshold of sleep, with its closed-in dreams, its smothered ambitions, and its cherished security. It was the place I belonged, the place I wanted to leave . . . the place I wanted to be. It was home. Heritage lies deep within these people and, no matter how great the desire to seek new places, no matter how far, the threads of their past bind them to this place of their youth.

Some years after my mother's death, I had occasion to return to my old home. While waiting alone near the familiar garden, I composed the following poem in memory of my mother.

September Garden

    I came face to face with time one day
        When morning sun dispelled September's haze,
    And cloud filled sky above the trees
        Canopied its rays.

    In the still of that familiar place
        I looked about for each remembered thing;
    All were there, though different, too, it seemed . . .
        As only time can bring.

CONCLUSION

A chorus of insects lent music to the hour,
   From bed of grass blanketed with dew;
The fading rose spilled petals at its feet,
   Where one time violets grew.

Borders once filled with flowers' fragrant bloom
   To weed and wild grass now had given way;
The garden bench where golden hours were spent
   Had fallen in decay.

A lingering robin, unaware of time,
   That blight September's garden would consume,
Foraged 'neath bending boughs where hung
   Crepe Myrtle's heavy bloom.

From its deep sleep of yesteryear,
   A purple aster roused to greet the morn;
I now was deep in all my yesteryears—
   Remembrances reborn.

Lost in time, the hours slipped gently by,
   With past recalled, each moment to reclaim;
Through the mist of memory then I seemed to hear
   My Mother call my name.

                        Sally Chinn Reisinger

A VIRGINIA VILLAGE